JJBun
Charlottesville
May / 1964

TAXES, LOOPHOLES AND MORALS

TAXES, LOOPHOLES AND MORALS

by Jerome R. Hellerstein

McGRAW-HILL BOOK COMPANY, INC.

New York   Toronto   London

TAXES, LOOPHOLES AND MORALS

FIRST EDITION

28074

To Pauline

ACKNOWLEDGMENTS

To the many persons who in one way or another contributed to this work, wittingly or unwittingly, including clients, students, and commentators on taxation, I express my deep appreciation. I am particularly indebted to my partner Victor Brudney for his comments and suggestions in reviewing the manuscript; to Professor Harold M. Groves of the University of Wisconsin, who was kind enough to read and comment on the chapters dealing with capital gains and the taxation of business; and to Sidney Prerau of the New York Bar for his suggestions concerning the chapter on charitable giving. I also wish to express my appreciation to my son David, who read several chapters of the work with the rigorous eye of a scientist, and to my secretary, Mrs. Alfreda Degheri, for the heavy typing burden which she carried so cheerfully.

Quotations from *Youngblood Hawke* by Herman Wouk. Reprinted by permission of the author.

Quotation from "Visit to the World of Expense Accounts" by Russell Lynes, *The New York Times*, February 24, 1957. Reprinted by permission. Copyright by *The New York Times*.

Quotations from "Report of Rabkin and Johnson's Federal Income, Gift and Estate Taxation," October, 1962. Reprinted by permission of Matthew Bender & Company.

Quotations from "The Myth of the Magic Expense Account" from _Dun's Review and Modern Industry_, August, 1960, pp. 39-40. Reprinted by permission of Dun & Bradstreet Publications Corporation.

Quotations from _Business Week_, August 1, 1953. Reprinted by permission of Business Week.

Quotations from "Reconsideration of the Capital Gains Tax—A Comment" by Raymond L. Richman, from _The National Tax Journal_, December, 1961. Reprinted by permission of the National Tax Association.

Quotations from _Mr. Justice Holmes and the Supreme Court_ by Felix Frankfurter. Reprinted by permission of The Belknap Press of Harvard University Press. Copyright 1938, 1961, by The President and Fellows of Harvard College.

Quotations from "Short Term and Other Income Tax Savings" by Paul F. Schwaighart, Jr., from _Trust and Estates Magazine_, May 1961. Reprinted by permission of Trust and Estates Magazine.

Quotations from "The Background of the Revenue Act of 1937" by Randolph Paul, from University of Chicago Law Review, 1937. Reprinted by permission of University of Chicago. Copyright 1937 by the University of Chicago Press.

Quotations from "Effects of Taxation on Executives" by Thomas H. Sanders. Reprinted by permission of Harvard University.

CONTENTS

Introduction

When I was a youngster growing up in a western city, my father used to tell a story, which I suspect was apocryphal, but which is worth repeating. One day, as he tells the tale, a stranger walked into the small jewelry store which my father operated and asked for the owner. He was directed to a back room which served as an office. He walked into the office, hung up his hat, and without a word sat himself in my father's swivel chair and put his feet up on the desk. My astonished father demanded, "Who are you?" "Your partner," was the reply. "I've come to check on whether you've paid me my share of the profits of the business," and he flashed his Internal Revenue Agent's badge.

About thirty years later I was sitting in my own home in Manhattan, being prodded by my daughter about my work as a tax lawyer. She was home from college on vacation and was asking probing questions. "How can you, with your liberal political views, devote most of your life to helping corporations take advantage of the loopholes and preferences in the tax law that I've so often heard you rail against?"

During the 1940s, I was working as tax counsel for the trustees in a bankruptcy reorganization of the top company of a large corporate pyramid. One Sunday morning I made a speech on taxation over a small Brooklyn radio station, in which I recommended an increase in corporate tax rates and a lowering of personal income-tax exemptions. This was such an obscure station that I doubted whether anyone was listening, other than my family and a few friends whom I had alerted to the broadcast. But in the unseen radio audience there was a large bondholder of the corporation whose tax work I was handling. He was furious over my speech and indignantly telephoned one of the trustees, urging him to fire me, since with my views I was in his mind unfit to act as tax counsel to a large corporation. Happily for me, the trustee was a man of stature and tolerance, who took the position that he was concerned only with my competence in handling the company's tax affairs, not with my views or activities as a citizen with respect to tax policy.

These three experiences in a sense underlie the writing of this book. If Uncle Sam was my father's involuntary partner in the twenties, he was very much a junior partner; with the steep increases in income-tax rates and the broadening of the tax base that have taken place in the intervening decades, the income tax has become a major factor in business and in the lives, not only of men of property, but also of millions of Americans of modest and middle incomes. At the same time, the tax law has grown into one of the most complex and refined statutes on the books, understood, if at all, only by those who devote most of their professional lives to studying its ramifications. No sophisticated business man these days will make a move without consulting his tax man. The consequence is that there has grown up at the bar a considerable number of lawyers who specialize in taxation.

Having been attracted to the tax field some twenty-five years ago, I have been confronted by the supposed conflicts of interest posed by my daughter and my radio-listener bondholder. The question pressed by my daughter is a variant of the accusation made against every criminal lawyer:

how can a lawyer with a conscience defend a man he believes to be guilty of the crime charged? The answer is that every man is entitled to his day in court, defended by a competent and dedicated lawyer. Unless we provide such defense, neither men's liberty nor their property will be secure. Unfortunately, we fail badly in this area, particularly with respect to our less privileged classes, minority groups, and dissident members of society, and the daily miscarriages of justice in our criminal courts bear witness to the need to provide all men with adequate defense.

By the same token, if we are to have a society governed by law, men are entitled to the benefits of all our laws, including those many of us regard as unfair or unwise, until we change them. We ought not confuse the lawyer's role in pressing a man's rights under the existing law with his tenets as to whether the law is just or wise. A lawyer who contests a New York divorce suit by showing that his client did not commit adultery—the only ground for divorce in that state—is not by that defense to be regarded as approving the state's restrictive divorce laws. A lawyer who defends a client's right under the tax law to deduct as a business expense the cost of an African safari, as one lawyer successfully did in the Tax Court, is not to be taken as thereby espousing the wisdom of the law in allowing lavish personal and entertainment expenses as deductions. Such a doctrine of guilt by association of the lawyer with the legal positions pressed for clients, is as offensive as the recent tendency to brand as a Soviet sympathizer a lawyer who defends a Communist in claiming the Fifth Amendment privilege against self-incrimination. If we proclaim the right, and indeed the duty, of American lawyers to represent without reproach the Peter Zengers, the Scottsboro boys, and the Communists, we must likewise reject the "guilt by client" branding of lawyers (as the noted trial lawyer Edward Bennett Williams calls it), when a liberal lawyer represents big business in an antitrust, a labor or a tax case—even when he's well-paid to do it.

The irate bondholder likewise suffered from a misconception of the lawyer's role. He demands complete identification of the lawyer with the client, soul as well as body, as part of his retainer. On the occasions when I have run into this attitude, and I am happy to report that it has been rare, I have responded by telling the client a story of the editor of an independent newspaper in my home town. He was a hardheaded, tough-minded newspaper man, who carried on vigorous crusades against political corruption and fought for civic improvement. Periodically, he received angry telephone calls from large advertisers who had been hurt by his campaigns, and who usually wound up with a threat to cancel their advertising. The editor's characteristic reply was, "Advertising, did you say? You've got the wrong department; I have nothing to do with advertising; I'll switch you to that department." A lawyer's political views and activities are his own private "editorial department," which I believe no client can properly transgress.

Consequently, I reject the reproaches of both my daughter and the irate bondholder as based on a misconception of a lawyer's role. And that is why I suffer no twinge of conscience when I stand before a New York University class in Washington Square during the morning and criticize judicial decisions giving their imprimatur to a tax-avoidance device, and then in the afternoon go down to Wall Street and set up the same device to save taxes for a client. Nor do I concede the right of any client to resent my espousing in this work any view which, if enacted into law, might increase his tax burdens. These are the hallmarks of an independent bar in a democracy.

In this volume, I am impinging on one of the most troublesome problems in a democratic society. Citizens face an almost impossible task in dealing with many of the major political and economic issues of our time. Whether it's the life-and-death issues of nuclear bomb testing and disarmament, how to handle the increasingly serious problems of automation and unemployment, or how to deal with tax controversies, the layman is bewildered. The problems are inordinately complicated; the facts are hard to get at; the experts in every field disagree. How is the intelligent layman to formulate views on these complex, confusing, yet critical issues? How should he vote when one candidate presses the need for big cuts in corporate taxes, while another plugs for increasing personal exemptions? Unless laymen have before them nontechnical works which give them the key facts, pose the critical issues and present the alternatives, they are lost in acting as responsible citizens in a democracy. This work is a modest try at presenting some of the key income-tax issues in a way that the intelligent layman will be able to understand, along with one man's views as to how they ought to be resolved in refashioning our income tax.

CHAPTER 1

A Lesson in History: How the Income
Tax Grew Up

One day while Justice Oliver Wendell Holmes, Jr., one of
the most highly venerated minds ever to grace the United
States Supreme Court bench, was filling out his income tax
return, his law clerk spoke up, "Mr. Justice, don't you hate
to pay taxes?" The learned Justice retorted, "No, young
feller, I like to pay taxes; with them I buy civilization." This
noble attitude toward taxation is not shared by many of
our citizens. As President Franklin D. Roosevelt wrote in
a message to Congress in 1937, "Too many individuals,
however, want the civilization at a discount." Indeed, one
anonymous wit is reported to have replied to Justice
Holmes' remark, "I think I have bought enough civilization
for my lifetime."

Most of us use every weapon and device at our command
to reduce our share of the tax burden. We use political pressure to shift the tax load to others; tax lobbying is a major
task of virtually every trade association and labor organization in Washington. Some of the most highly paid legal
and accounting talent of the country devotes its unrelenting
effort and imagination to finding ways of reducing the tax
bills of clients. And cheating on business and entertainment expenses and other deductions is so widely hon-
ored an annual exercise when tax time rolls around, that the
citizen who can cut corners with Uncle Sam and fails to
do so is regarded as a "sucker." A lament of millions of

lower-bracket taxpayers is their lack of any chance to emulate business and professional men in chiseling on taxes.

The Federal income tax has always aroused strong passions. It had its origin during the Civil War, when it was reluctantly presented to Congress as a "disagreeable duty," forced by the threat of "the annihilation of this government." And it began modestly enough, at rates of 3 per cent to 10 per cent, without hint of the stature it would attain. The Civil War income tax was distinctly a rich man's tax; it affected only 1 per cent of the population.

When the war ended, great pressure was brought to kill this odious measure, which had been justified only by the exigencies of war. The Chairman of the House Ways and Means Committee attacked the principle of graduation of rates according to incomes as offensive to the "republican form of government," and held that it could "only be defended on the same ground that the highwayman defends his acts." The tax was allowed to expire in 1870.

Nearly two decades passed in which the income tax was not a serious political issue. True, the Socialist Party and the agrarian groups which were the heart of the Populist Party, made platform demands for a progressive income tax; but the general prosperity of the country during the eighties prevented these voices from being listened to with much sympathy. However, the nineties brought hard times for the Western wheat grower and the Southern cotton planter. The collision between the industrial and financial centers—where large fortunes were being built and new large combinations of capital were growing in power—and the West and the South brought increased clamor for the income tax. The tax systems of the states and local governments relied heavily on the property tax; farmers and others in rural areas were bearing taxes on their land and visible personal property. The rich urban investor in stocks and bonds, the business man and the professional man were shouldering little of the tax burden. The income tax was the device to tax these growing wealthy groups that were escaping their fair share of the tax burden.

The Democratic presidential victory of 1892 was in part a result of a widespread belief that fiscal reform was needed to eliminate tax inequalities and injustices. When President Cleveland proposed an income tax to Congress in 1893, a fierce storm of protest broke out. Senator John Sherman declared:

"In a republic like ours, where all men are equal, this attempt to array the rich against the poor or the poor against the rich is socialism, communism and devilism."

Another senator denounced the levy as a scheme devised by "the professors with their books, the socialists with their schemes" and "the anarchists with their bombs."

The advocates of the levy were equally fervent in the grandiloquent picture they painted of what the tax would mean to the country. Congressman De Armond of Missouri rose to these heights:

"The passage of the bill will mark the dawn of a brighter day, with more sunshine, more of the songs of birds, more of that sweetest music, the laughter of children well fed, well clothed, well housed. . . . God hasten the era of equality in taxation and in opportunity."

An income tax levied at a uniform 2 per cent rate on income over $4,000 was passed; but the fates denied the country the opportunity—at least in the nineties—to test out either the dire fears of Senator Sherman or the glowing hopes of Congressman De Armond. The victory of the income-tax

supporters was short-lived, for the Supreme Court, in a
sharply divided decision, held the tax unconstitutional. The
major ground for invalidating the levy was that it was declared to be a "direct tax," a tax which Congress could not
impose under the Constitution without apportioning it
according to the population of the states. And so the income tax had to await another two decades of political agitation before the Sixteenth Amendment to the Constitution was adopted in 1913, explicitly giving Congress the
power to impose income taxes without apportionment.

The income tax became a symbol of reform among
agrarian and labor groups throughout the West and the
South. The turn of the century was marked by bitter conflict between the Northeastern industrial centers and the
agrarian West and South. This was the period of the emer-
gence of powerful capitalists and of the building of great
fortunes, of the prominence of the trusts—the beef trust,
the oil trust, and the sugar trust.

Farmers, debt-ridden, suffering from declining prices,
workers tasting the first bitter fruits of industrialization,
and social reformers and small businessmen discriminated
against by railroads and crushed by rising big business, all
joined in the Populist movement to demand antitrust legislation, tariff reduction, railroad regulation, free silver and
the income tax. Yet, by one of the most ironic twists of
political events in American history, it was a conservative
Republican President, William Howard Taft, and a rock-
ribbed Republican Congress which submitted the income-
tax amendment to the states for adoption. The demand
for an income tax—a levy that was detested by the Republican leadership—was injected into the bitter Congressional
debates over tariff reform in 1909. The Democrats, supported by a group of insurgent Young Republicans from

the West, including La Follette of Wisconsin and Borah of Idaho, succeeded in placing President Taft in a position where he felt compelled by the political dynamics of a tense congressional and intraparty fight to call for the submission of an income-tax amendment. The Republican Party leaders viewed Taft's action as a brilliant strategic move, designed to head off wide popular demand for a new income-tax law and to heal the party's strife. It was grounded in the expectation that the amendment would be defeated among the states.

This over-clever move backfired; while only one state, Alabama, ratified the amendment in 1909, by February 3, 1913, the requisite three-fourths of the states had approved the amendment. Thereby, the Republicans found themselves the unhappy progenitors of what, from a conservative point of view, was their most illegitimate, their most errant and indisputably their most prodigal child—the detested graduated income tax.

Like most institutions, the income tax developed modestly. The first act passed by Congress in 1913, under its new constitutional power, levied a 1 per cent normal tax on all incomes above personal exemptions of $4,000 for married persons and $3,000 for single persons; and a surtax beginning at 1 per cent on incomes of $20,000 to $50,000 and rising to a top rate of 6 per cent on incomes over $500,000.

No great changes took place in the income tax until America entered World War I. Indeed, to a very large extent, wars tell the story of the giant steps in our income tax—it was born in the Civil War, it first reached the levels of a modern, steeply graduated levy in World War I and it was revolutionized in World War II. Heavy wartime budgets, inflation and vastly expanded public services; these are at the roots of the history of the income tax.

By the time World War I ended, exemptions had been reduced to $2,000 for married persons and family heads and to $1,000 for single persons; and surtax rates had reached a high of 65 per cent on incomes over $100,000. Yet, a married man with two dependents having an income of $25,000 paid only $2,850 in tax; and only five and one-half million returns were filed out of a population of 106 million people.

In 1921, with the conflagration ended, a war-weary country, which experienced declining production while the cost of living was still rising, swept into the White House Warren G. Harding, with a Republican Congress to back him. Andrew W. Mellon, the "greatest Secretary of the Treasury since Alexander Hamilton," immediately set out to cut income-tax rates, particularly in the higher levels. By the time Calvin Coolidge "did not choose to run" for re-election in 1928, the top surtax rates had been cut from the wartime high of 65 per cent to 20 per cent on incomes over $100,000. At the same time exemptions for a married couple were raised to $3,500, for a single person to $1,500, with a $400 exemption for each dependent. The size of the 1928 income tax is indicated by the fact that the tax on a family of four with a $10,000 income had dwindled to $83.

The depression of the thirties sharply reduced national income and turned the budgetary surpluses of the twenties into deficits. With the coming of the New Deal and the adoption of measures to take care of the unemployed and to broaden public services, there were some increases in income-tax rates, particularly at the higher levels, while personal exemptions were lowered.

It was World War II, however, that revolutionized the income tax and gave the levy its essential present-day characteristics. For the first time in our history, the tax which had been an exclusively comfortable and rich-man's tax, became a broad-based levy extended to the masses of the population, coupled with steep starting rates and rapid graduation to new high rates. Thus, for 1940, there were filed seven and one-half million returns reporting taxable income, at a time when the country's population was at 132 million. By 1960 there were forty-eight million taxable returns filed (sixty million income tax returns were filed in all) out of a population of 180 million. In 1940, rates began at 4 per cent and rose to 79 per cent; in 1962, they began at 20 per cent and went as high as 91 per cent. In 1940, a married man with two children paid a tax of $75 on a $5,000 income, whereas in 1962 he paid $520. In 1940, he paid a tax of $3,570 on a $25,000 income, and in 1962 his tax was $6,300. At $100,000 of income, the 1942 tax of $43,000 had risen to $52,000.

One other significant development took place as a result of this refashioning of the income tax during World War II; for most taxpayers the income tax lost its most distinctive characteristic as a graduated levy. More than three out of five taxpayers—those who form the great base of lower incomes in our national income pyramid—paid a flat, ungraduated tax for 1960 of 20 per cent on all their taxable incomes. This ungraduated levy accounted for $9.3 billions, or about one-fourth of the entire income tax collected for the year. The hardships to lower-income families imposed by a flat 20 per cent tax on the first $2,000 of income above current low-level personal exemptions of $600 a person induced the Treasury in 1963 to recommend that rates on the first $1,000 of taxable income be reduced to 14 per cent. Under this proposal the top rate of 91 per cent would be cut back to the World War I top rate of 65 per cent, and the rates would be reduced all along the line for various income brackets.

This shift in the income tax from a levy on the rich and the comfortable to a mass tax with a broad base, including a large segment of the working class, was brought about, not only by changes in the tax law, but also by rising incomes and inflation. A rapid and inflationary rise in incomes pushed millions of persons higher in taxable income brackets. Thus, the average weekly earnings in manufacturing industries in 1940 were $24.96; in 1962 they were $96.56. Adjusting the 1940 earnings to 1962 prices, the 1940 earnings amounted to $53.91, as compared with 1962 earnings of $96.56.

The defenders of the privileged classes fought the income tax bitterly at its inception and were realistic and farsighted in seeing at least some of the implications of the tax to men of wealth. Thus, when Joseph H. Choate successfully fought the 1894 levy in the courts, he condemned the 2 per cent tax as "communistic in its purposes and tendencies," and thunderously told the Supreme Court that if it upheld the nefarious income-tax law, it might within five years, if "this communistic march goes on," be forced to uphold at some later time "a tax of 20 per cent on all incomes in excess of $20,000." His dreary predictions were doubtless dismissed by many as the fantasy of a prejudiced mind, but this one has come true with a vengeance.

On the other hand, the vast growth of the underbelly of the ravenous levy into a tax on the masses was an ironic twist of history, which neither Choate nor the zealous advocates of the tax could foresee. Who could have predicted that this darling of agrarian groups, of labor unions and liberals, this great instrument for taxing and redistributing the wealth of the capitalists, would become a broadly based levy, with billions of dollars a year collected from lower-income taxpayers? If Choate were capable of finding anything at all amusing in this instrument of the devil, he must be chuckling in his grave over the loud complaints against the income tax now being made by the descendants of its most ardent devotees, who now call for higher exemptions, reduction and refinement in the first brackets, and an easing of the burdens of the levy on their constituents.

CHAPTER 2

A Grand Delusion: The Appearance and Reality of High-Bracket Rates

While for most taxpayers the income tax has lost its distinctive character as a graduated levy geared to differences in ability to pay, for the most affluent, the rate scale is unmistakably graduated, and at high-income levels the rates are severely steep. Nevertheless, the rate schedule is a colossal delusion. Our affluent taxpayers, as a rule, just don't pay taxes on their incomes at the high scheduled rates. And the reason is that our tax laws are full of leaks, loopholes, exemptions and preferences.

If we consider the taxes that would be collected from upper-level taxpayers, if the rate schedule were actually applied to the incomes of our more comfortable taxpayers, and then look at what they really pay, we find the comparison highly illuminating. For 1956, the last year for which detailed studies are available, the average income-tax bill paid by all individuals with incomes of $100,000 or more, amounted to approximately 36 per cent of their incomes. Yet, the tax tables call for an effective tax rate of about 67 per cent applied to a $100,000 income of an individual; at $200,000 the effective rate would be about 78 per cent, and at $500,000 it would be 80 per cent. The taxes actually paid by persons in these brackets are probably considerably less than half the rates indicated by the tables. The explanation for this sharp discrepancy lies in the fact that the tax law contains a number of exemptions and preferences which inure primarily to the benefit of upper-bracket taxpayers.

The tax base has leaks in it. Some income is exempt from tax by law; some types of income are granted preferential rates of tax; and some classes of taxpayers are the beneficiaries of preferred rates. Finally, deductions of a dubious character effectively reduce high incomes.

Let us look at each of these sieves in the tax structure.

A major legal gap in the income-tax base affecting upper-bracket incomes is tax-exempt income. An investor in bonds or other securities issued by a state or local government is not taxable on the interest from the bonds. This exemption was placed in the law in 1913 and has been there ever since. It grew out of a Congressional fear that such a tax might be unconstitutional; the legislators thought that the Federal government might be interfering with the sovereign borrowing power of the states and their local subdivisions by taxing the income on the bonds they issued. Although the exemption for State and local bond interest is regarded, in the words of Assistant Secretary of the Treasury Stanley Surrey and by many other students of the subject, as "indefensible from the standpoint of income-tax policy," the Treasury's repeated efforts to repeal it have failed because of the spirited opposition of State and local governments, bankers and others.

It is an easy tax refuge, which is widely recommended by tax advisers for the wealthy taxpayer. Banks and investment houses regularly send their wealthy clients appealing tables showing how net income after taxes can be doubled or trebled by shifting to tax-exempts. Thus a $1,000, 5 per cent bond of a utility company will yield a taxpayer in the 80 per cent bracket $10 a year after taxes; by buying a state or local bond, which may pay only 3½ per cent interest, the taxpayer will wind up with $35 a year after taxes, an increase in his net return after taxes of 250 per cent. And at the

50 per cent tax bracket, the rate of return on the 3½ per cent tax-exempt bond would be 40 per cent above the 2½ per cent yield of the corporate bond, after taxes. Almost $600 million in income escaped tax through this hatch in 1957; and the major share of this income naturally goes to persons in the middle and upper brackets. Undoubtedly, the taxes escaped through the purchase of exempt bonds are rising sharply as states and municipalities increase their school and general construction programs and other expenditures, and hence their borrowings.

The income-tax law is based on the principle that in order to produce *equality of tax burden* we need *inequality in tax rates;* that as a man's income goes up, his ability to pay taxes increases, and rates ought to rise. One of the deepest cuts in the actual tax bill of higher income taxpayers grows out of the reversal of this principle in the case of capital gains. Profits from sales of stocks, bonds, real estate and other properties are taxed at lower rates than income generally. Naturally, the upper and middle-bracket taxpayers own most of the property in the country; consequently, they generate the capital gains (and losses). A study based on net long-term capital gains (the excess of gains over losses) of $3.7 billion reported in 1957 income-tax returns (only one-half the actual gain was required to be reported) estimates that $1.4 billion of additional taxes would have been payable if these profits were taxed in the same way as income generally. Treasury reports for later years show that net long-term capital gains reached an all-time high of $4.2 billion in 1959 and dropped to $3.8 billion in 1960.

Dividends are also preferred income under the tax law. A stockholder need not report at all the first $50 of dividends, and a husband and wife may pay no tax on $100 of dividends. Moreover, the rate on the dividends that are taxed is cut by 4 per cent below the rates on incomes generally. The dividend exclusion exempted from tax in 1960 some $380 million in dividends, and the 4 per cent tax credit cut taxes of stockholders by about $300 million. Stock ownership is concentrated in higher level taxpayers, so that most of the benefits of this preferential treatment goes to high-bracket taxpayers, mainly those with incomes above $10,000. The 1960 figures show that about 70 per cent of the $300 million in tax cuts due to the dividend tax credit went to persons with incomes over $10,000; and in addition, these taxpayers excluded from income about $160 million of the $380 million of dividends exempted from tax by the $50 exclusion.

The split-income system, under which a married man's earnings and other income are treated as having been received for tax purposes equally by himself and his wife, is a major factor in reducing the impact of high rates. Thus, if an unmarried man had an income of $18,000 in 1962, he would pay a tax of $6,200. If he were married and had the same income, it would be split for tax purposes between himself and his wife; there would be two incomes of $9,000 each; the tax on the two $9,000 incomes would produce a total tax of only $4,600.

The story back of the split-income system is a telling lesson in practical politics. Arizona, California, Idaho, Louisiana, Nevada, New Mexico, Washington, Texas, and other states, influenced by Spanish law, treat husband and wife as a community, under which earnings and income from certain classes of property belong equally to husband and wife. That is not true of most states, which are governed by the common-law property system inherited from England. Taxpayers residing in community-property states succeeded in getting the Supreme Court to rule that, since half a man's earnings belong as a matter of property law to his wife, he should pay tax on only his half and she on her half of the income. It was by no means either a necessary or a desirable result that tax rules ought to follow local property rules; and the decision was widely criticized by commentators. But it was the law, with the result that there was a considerable advantage to middle and upper-bracket married persons living in the community-property states.

This produced discrimination against married taxpayers living in New York and Massachusetts and other common-law states. The Legislatures of a number of traditional common-law states—Michigan, Nebraska, Oklahoma and Pennsylvania—decided to get on the Federal gravy train for their citizens (it cost the states nothing), and adopted legislation purporting to adopt a community-property system. This was too much for the staid Pennsylvania Supreme Court, which held the law unconstitutional; but it worked in other states. At the same time, there was a good deal of agitation to eliminate this unfairness through Congressional action, by taxing the income of a married taxpayer entirely to the income earner or property owner in the community-property states. This proposal met the solid opposition of the senators and congressmen from the community-property states.

To eliminate the discrimination between married persons living in the common-law states and the community-property states, Congress moved in the opposite direction in 1948 and amended the income-tax law so as to give couples in all states the benefits of splitting their incomes. This move was widely hailed as producing equality among taxpayers in the various states, and was also supported by groups ready to back any technique which would reduce taxes in higher brackets.

The split-income system has never benefited most taxpayers. If a taxpayer's income does not bring him above the first bracket, after personal exemptions and deductions, it makes no difference in his tax liability whether or not he splits it with his wife. The entire income is still taxed at the first bracket rate. But if the taxpayer's income rises into higher brackets, his tax bill may be sharply reduced by the split-income system. In fact, for the year 1948, when the split-income system was adopted, only about 22 per cent of all married couples were benefited; 97 per cent of the dollar benefits in tax reduction went to 5 per cent of all married taxpayers. Using 1956 figures (the latest year for which a study has been made), 76 per cent of the benefits of income-tax splitting went to persons with incomes over $8,000. And the split-income system has made a deep cut in over-all tax collections; it reduced taxes for 1956 by approximately $3.8 billion.

The major benefits under the split-income system are in the middle-to-high brackets—not the lowest or the highest brackets. Thus, using 1962 rates, the major benefits are in the $10,000 to $100,000 range; at $24,000 the highest relative tax reduction occurs—at this point married couples pay 29 per cent less than single persons with the same incomes, at $50,000, there is a 24 per cent saving, at $100,000, a 20 per cent saving, while at $400,000, the saving declines to about 7½ per cent.

There are those who advocate the repeal of the split-income system and the taxation of the income recipient in all states, including community-property tax states, at full rates, a proposal which at least a good many lawyers believe would be constitutional. But these are voices crying in the wilderness. Few congressmen, even if they thought the proposal sound, would risk supporting a tax increase affecting their most vocal and politically effective constituents. So the split-income system is now part of the fabric of our tax system. Indeed, this is the case with most tax-reducing provisions; it is virtually impossible to dislodge them once they have become a part of our income-tax system.

While tax-cutting provisions are hard to dislodge, they tend to fan out and bring other tax reductions in their wake. Once the split-income system was adopted for married taxpayers, others had a strong basis for claiming they were being discriminated against. How about the widow or the widower who has to support a family and perhaps hire a housekeeper to look after the household? Why should such a person pay a higher rate than his married neighbor? There was a good deal of appeal in this plea; Congress responded by cutting the rates for heads of households to a point about halfway between the married couple and the single perso This was further refined to give a widow or widower w maintains a household, with at least one child as dependent, the benefit of split-income rates for two years after the death of the spouse; this too was a readjustment in the interest of equity. These proliferations and extensions are characteristic of the tax law; once a change is instituted, there are usually other groups of taxpayers who can make out an appealing case for getting in under the same umbrella. All this reduces the effective rates and, incidentally, helps to complicate the tax law. Indeed, many of the complications and refinements of the income tax grow out of a laudable desire to do equity among taxpayers more or less similarly situated.

In a recent brilliant essay on "Ideologies in Taxation," Louis Eisenstein has dubbed percentage depletion, "the special deduction for imaginary costs." This remarkable leak in the tax structure is reserved for taxpayers in the oil and gas industries, in coal mining and in other kinds of mining.

It is in no small measure responsible for a considerable crop of Texas millionaires.

Percentage depletion stems, like most preferences in the tax law, from an unassailable principle, one that applies equally to all taxpayers. If you spend $1,000 for a machine used in your manufacturing business and the machine lasts five years, you are presumably using up the machine at the rate of $200 a year and are entitled to $200 a year as a depreciation deduction against your income. Or, if you pay $1,000 for the right to mine coal for 10 years, and expect to take out one-fifth of the coal each year, you are entitled to a depletion deduction of $200 against the sales price of the coal to your customers, or against other income. This is the so-called straight-line method of handling depreciation or depletion. There are other methods, but in one way or another, they are devices for allowing taxpayers to deduct the actual costs of doing business. But nowhere, except in the preferred natural-resources industries, is a taxpayer permitted to deduct as an expense of doing business, during the life of the property, more than its cost (tax basis).

Because it is extremely difficult, even for the most carefully trained mining engineers, to estimate with any degree of accuracy the amount of oil, coal, copper, clay or other mineral or material that will come out of the ground, a method was developed for allowing a part of the selling price of each ton of coal, each barrel of oil or each load of gravel, etc., as a depletion deduction. This method tended to tie in the tax allowances with the production of income. So far, this was merely a way of solving a difficult engineering problem and produced no basic preference over other taxpayers. Then, the oil and mining interests pressed further. They claimed that their industries ought to be given special treatment in the national interest; they argued that their business is very hazardous, that in exploring for new sources, again and again they strike dry holes, and that if our natural resources are to be developed, special tax treatment is needed. In more recent times, the argument has been pressed that we must have oil to protect our war machine, defend our country and win the cold war. Congress, vigorously goaded by senators and congressmen from Texas, Louisiana, Utah, Pennsylvania, California and other oil and gas and mining states, yielded and adopted the extraordinary rule that taxpayers in these industries could keep on deducting depletion costs *long after they had recovered in their tax returns the entire cost of the properties!*

The result is that every time a barrel of oil is sold, 27½ per cent of the proceeds are deductible, as are 23 per cent of the proceeds from lead, nickel and zinc, 10 per cent of the proceeds from coal, and so on, as long as nature yields up her rich products. There is a case on record in which one individual oil operator had total net income of $14 million over a five-year period, but paid a total of only $80,000 in income taxes; his effective rate of tax because of percentage depletion (and the related intangible drilling costs allowable) was six-tenths of 1 per cent.

These, then, and other leaks in income, rate preferences and special benefits help account for the striking differences between the appearance of a steeply-graduated rate structure and the actual tax payments made by the more comfortable members of our society. There are, of course, other leaks in our tax system which are not authorized by law, such as hundreds of millions of dollars of dividend and interest income that go unreported each year and large amounts of personal and entertainment expenses that are deducted as business expenses. We shall consider these items elsewhere in this work.

Many staunch supporters of the provisions of the tax law that we have been considering, as well as others who would eliminate many of these preferences, are also troubled by provisions which affect the low and middle-bracket taxpayer. If we actually collected income taxes on all earned income, and on all income from business and property after deducting business expenses, but without allowing any exemptions or other deductions, we would collect annually many billions of dollars more in income taxes than we do now. For example, one economist has estimated that if we taxed social security payments, unemployment insurance, workmen's compensation, veterans' benefits and similar items, nearly $10 billion of income would be added to the tax base. Using 1957 figures, tax collections would have risen by about $2 billion. For the same year, if we did not allow any personal nonbusiness deductions (the standard deduction of 10 per cent of adjusted gross income up to $1,000; or, if the standard deduction is not used, if we disallowed real-estate taxes on personal residences, interest on nonbusiness loans, charitable contributions, medical-expense deductions and so forth) the tax base would have gone up by $26 billion and income-tax collections would have risen by $5.7 billion. One could go on and figure out how much would be gained by the Treasury by eliminating the extra exemption of $600 for the aged and the blind, the child-care credit and so forth. The great bulk of these items principally affect people in very modest income brackets.

All this might seem like an idle exercise in statistics and higher mathematics, since it seems pretty remote that Congress would tax social security benefits and unemployment insurance, and eliminate virtually all the tax deductions the wage earner and salaried man receive. But such proposals are being seriously made by those who emphasize the need to stop the erosion of the tax base, as a way of making possible the lowering of tax rates. True, they are often urged by spokesmen for business and propertied groups, who are at the same time staunch defenders of the leaks and preferences that inure to the benefit of the higher-bracket taxpayers. But such proposals have also been supported by more disinterested students of taxation, who would eliminate many of the upper-bracket special privileges as well, and reduce our stiff rate schedule.

To equate all erosions of the tax base, to lump together the exemption for social security payments and the exemption for interest on state and local bonds, to consider the standard deduction alongside percentage depletion, is to use a bulldozer approach to tax reform. Obviously, no such broad-sweep approach can make sense. Each exemption, privilege or deduction must be examined on its own merits. It may be sound social policy to retain the exemption for social security payments, while eliminating the exemption for interest on state and local bond issues. Perhaps the deduction for real estate taxes on residences should be repealed, but it by no means necessarily follows that the medical-expense deduction should also be repealed. Rational tax reform will not be accomplished by seeking to eliminate all personal deductions, all exemptions and all preferences in one fell swoop. Some erosions of the tax base may be eminently desirable as a matter of social policy.

And the question as to whose ox would be gored is of great importance in making a judgment as to what's good for the country. It may make a crucial difference to determine whether a particular shoring up of the tax base would raise the tax load of the three out of five taxpayers in the lowest bracket, or the taxes of those in the middle or highest brackets. Or the decisive issue may not lie in the realm of income levels and equity among taxpayers at all. We may find it appropriate to ignore these factors, if there are overriding economic considerations, if the proper functioning of the economy, or the needs of the cold war dictate the grant of preferential tax treatment. In short, each leak in the tax base, each exemption, each area of preferential treatment in the tax law must be examined on its own merits and in the context of its impact on the national interest, if we are to refashion our income-tax law wisely.

CHAPTER 3

Capital Gains: The Bargain Basement
of the Income Tax

Equality in taxation of income is, as we have seen, deliberately rejected by the key feature of progressive income taxation—that tax rates should rise as income rises. But within given income brackets, the equality principle remains a much to be desired goal of the income tax—a goal to be achieved unless there are compelling reasons for creating further inequalities between taxpayers. Probably the most far-reaching line drawn between taxpayers in the same brackets grows out of the differences in the treatment of income from property and income from services. And the preference of property over man finds its major expression in the treatment of capital gains.

If you own a piece of land, or a building, or a car dealership, or stocks, or bonds and they have gone up in value since you bought them, when you sell, the profit on the sale is taxed as a capital gain. And if you held the property over six months, you never pay more than a 25 per cent tax on the profit; and you may pay less, because you report only half of the profits, or pay a 25 per cent tax on the full profit, whichever produces the lower tax. Thus, if you're in the 30 per cent bracket, you'll include half the profit at full rates, and pay a 15 per cent tax on the profit; but if you're in the 60 per cent bracket, you'll pay at the 25 per cent rate on the whole profit. Under the Treasury's 1963 tax-reduction proposals, only 30 per cent of the profit

28

would be includible in income and the ceiling rate on the whole profit would be cut to 19.5 per cent.

This preferred treatment of capital gains is a sore point for many in our tax system. Doctors, lawyers, accountants, writers and TV actors typically have no way of avoiding high rates on their incomes. But they hear business men boast about their deals in property. Whether it's a business with a profitable new product that's been sold, or a piece of real estate that was bought at just the right time and is now being disposed of at a handsome profit, only a capital gain tax results. This is a widespread occurrence. The number of small businesses that have grown and been sold for large sums, the soaring prices in the real estate market, the decades of inflation in the stock market—all this has produced a society in which a considerable body of favored taxpayers have had large profits on which the tax ceiling has been 25 per cent.

From a sociological viewpoint, there is a good deal to be said for more severe taxation of profit from appreciation in the value of property than from personal-service income. Increases in the value of real estate over the years are due primarily to the community, not the efforts of the individual owner. The population explosion, the development of schools, highways, airports, railroads and parks in the neighborhood, and the entire community growth, to which a particular owner of real estate will ordinarily have contributed little, are typically major factors in real estate rises. Likewise, the growth of many industries and increases in the value of their stocks are to a very large extent the result of general community factors; aircraft and many electronics manufacturers owe their growth largely to the existence of the cold war; the expansion of automobile and telephone and electric utility companies grew out of an affluent society; and the boom in the building trades and the related home furnishings industry owes much to governmental housing subsidies and loans.

While it is undoubtedly true that particular inventors, engineers, financiers and others in management have made essential contributions to the growth of particular companies and industries, nevertheless, the fact remains indisputable—as Henry George so methodically and effectively demonstrated—that much of the value involved in capital gains realized on sales of businesses and real estate and stocks and bonds is created by society. Society may, therefore, have a legitimate claim for heavier taxation of capital gains of individuals, than of other income. And there was a time in our tax law when earned income was preferred; we had a special 10 per cent credit for earned income up to $14,000.

There are, however, vigorous supporters of the preferential treatment of profits from sales of securities and other investment assets. The doctor, the lawyer, the accountant, the architect are paid for their services. They are selling no assets; hence they are subject to ordinary income-tax rates. Similarly, when the manufacturer sells his product or the merchant his wares, or a builder of houses sells a block of one-family homes, the profits are taxed as ordinary income, not capital gain. However, when you go outside the service or stock-in-trade areas, you are dealing, we are told, with the fixed assets of the business—such as plant and machinery or investments in real estate, stocks and bonds. Any profit made on a sale of such items is not regular business income and ought not be taxed as such. Indeed, some countries do not impose any tax on the profits from sales of such capital assets; that's true generally in Canada and Australia and was true in England until 1962, when the law was changed to tax short-term gains. And the reason given is that such appreciation in the value of such assets is not income at all. Besides, this type of profit may be the result of many years of appreciation; to tax the whole profit in the year of sale at regular progressive rates would produce an unfair piling up of the tax burden.

Finally, it is argued that the lowered rates and the ceiling on capital gains are essential to our economy. If we didn't have a special capital gains rate, people would not invest the funds required to keep our economy healthy and growing; the whole country gains through new jobs, and new plants and expanded industry. Indeed, those who argue that there should not even be a 25 or 19.5 per cent tax, purport to demonstrate that the business expansion that would follow a lifting of the tax would produce more business revenue for the Treasury than the capital gains tax.

Once having adopted a distinction between gains from the sale of "capital assets" as they are called—which produce the magic capital gain—and other income, a mad scramble inevitably developed to fall within the favored area. Now, it's pretty hard for a doctor or a lawyer to be selling anything, let alone capital assets. But the writers thought they could fall under the capital gains umbrella, since they sell property; the law calls it "literary property." The courts agreed that writers can "sell" property, but refused to grant the authors capital gains treatment because they concluded that writers are in the business of selling literary property; hence they are like the car or shoe manufacturer who sells his product. Consequently, writers generally failed to come under the capital gains shelter.

Amateur writers, however, had a better case. When General Eisenhower sold his *Crusade in Europe*, he received a

ruling from the Treasury that because he was not a professional writer, he was not in the business of selling books and,
therefore, was entitled to the advantage of capital gains
treatment for the proceeds. This was a perfectly reasonable
ruling in the light of the law. However, the result in-
censed some congressmen; the Internal Revenue Code was
amended in 1950 by what is popularly known as "the
Eisenhower amendment," so that now amateur writers who
sell novels or essays or plays, are, like professional authors,
denied capital gains treatment. And the vicissitudes of
political fortunes produced the ironic twist that one of the
first victims of the Eisenhower amendment was President
Truman. When he sold his memoirs in 1953, he was unable
to obtain a capital gain; the Eisenhower amendment made
his fees ordinary income. President Truman did, however,
succeed in spreading the income over a five-year period.

While the writers were thus relegated to ordinary income
treatment, our scientifically minded society reflected a far
greater concern for the inventor. The inventor started in
much the same position as the writer in trying to reach the
Holy Grail of capital gains taxation. An invention is recognized by law as "property." If the owner is careful to "sell"
his invention and patents, not merely to "license" them, the
law is that he is selling property. This is of crucial technical importance, because you don't ever get your foot into
the door of the coveted capital gains structure unless you
are selling (or exchanging) an asset. Because licensing is
not sale, a license produces ordinary income. Inevitably,
there developed extensive litigation and a body of highly
esoteric knowledge, with refined distinctions that require
the combined learning of patent and tax experts, to chart a
reasonably safe course as to whether a "sale" or a "license"
has occurred. For example, may patent rights be "sold"

country by country, or to avoid "license," must worldwide rights be transferred? Is "sale" inconsistent with the common patent arrangement under which the inventor is paid a stated royalty for every article manufactured under the patent? These and numerous other variations produced highly technical and often unrealistic distinctions between sales and licenses.

Moreover, the professional inventor found himself faced with the barrier that debarred the professional writer from the exclusive capital gains circle. When he sells an invention, isn't the inventor selling "stock in trade," like the manufacturer selling his product or the writer disposing of a novel? The rules here were also bewildering, for the line between inventing as a hobby and as a profession was particularly difficult to draw. The courts held that one invention wasn't enough to move the creator from amateur to professional standing. Two inventions in some cases qualified for capital gains, but beyond that lurked danger. However, an inventor of an oil filter squeezed through on selling five patents because he sold them all in one deal, whereas if he had made five separate sales, he might have had ordinary income. Moreover, one might be a professional for some inventions and an amateur for others. A Princeton professor of physics was a professional inventor when he worked on acoustics and optics; but he was a mere amateur when he invented a gadget for grinding toothbrush bristles to help prevent "pink toothbrush."

Congress again stepped in to legislate, but instead of debarring amateur inventors from capital gains, as it did with writers, it reversed its approach and explicitly gave its approval to capital gains treatment for all inventors, amateur and professional. This happened in 1954 and was largely due to the cold war and to the prime importance placed by

Congress on encouraging invention and scientific progress.
The Congressional Committee that recommended this
privileged treatment for inventors said that it was designed
to "provide an incentive to inventors to contribute to the
welfare of the Nation" by assuring them capital gains treatment. Incidentally, some noninventors were let in on this
bonanza—people who finance inventors were also cut in on
the capital gains deal.

The investor and the inventor rank pretty much at the
top of the peak in Congress' scale of values, as reflected by
favored and disfavored tax treatment. The qualifying phrase
"pretty much" is deliberate, for I now come to the most
favored group of taxpayers, the highest caste capital gains
beneficiaries—corporate executives. Let me make it clear
that I am here talking about favored and disfavored taxpayers only in relation to capital gains versus ordinary income.
I would want to think long and hard before deciding which
class of taxpayers is the most favored in the income-tax law
as a whole. It would be hard, I think, to match in ultra-
favoritism the position of the "percentage depleters"; yet I
would hesitate to say that over-all they are higher in the tax
caste system than the corporate executive, with fringe benefits, expense accounts and stock options all combined. Of
course, given a well-treated corporate executive who also
owns interests in natural resources ventures and is therefore,
a percentage depleter, I should be willing to toss all caution
to the winds and unequivocally nominate him for that highest post—the No. 1 most privileged taxpayer in the bizarre
hierarchy of our taxation caste system.

The corporate executive is free to obtain from his corporation a part of the compensation for his services in the form
of capital gain. No sham or trick is required. It's all open

and aboveboard, because Congress deliberately opened this tax flood gate for this favored child. Writers, actors, prize fighters and others may tear their hair at high tax brackets and wear out the tax bar (albeit at high legal fees) seeking fancy schemes to avoid tax and sometimes succeed and sometimes fail. Groucho Marx and Jack Benny succeeded, as we shall see shortly, while poor Ingemar Johannsen failed. But corporate executives, like inventors since 1950, can live with the knowledge born of a secure complacency that Congress took good care of them.

There are two major techniques that are used to pay the corporate executive in capital gain currency—the stock option and the pension.

A corporation may give its executives an option to buy its shares at a discount of as much as 15 per cent *below its market value when the option is granted.* The option may run as long as ten years, so that the employee has a free ride on the market for that period. Although an option to buy shares of stock of a listed, growing corporation anytime over the next five or ten years at 85 per cent of its market price today can be very valuable, no tax is paid on the grant of the option. Nor does the employee pay any tax when he exercises the option and buys the stock. If at the time the option is granted, the discount price is no more than 5 per cent under the then market for the stock, the law postpones all tax until the stock is sold, and then the magic umbrella of the ceiling capital gains tax comes into play.

Where the discount price at the time the option is granted is more than 5 per cent but under 15 per cent of the then market, a slightly varied set of rules comes into play. Again, no income is taxed when the option is granted or when it is exercised. However, when the option stock is sold or transmitted to the employee's heirs or beneficiaries on his death, compensation income may result, but it cannot exceed the original 15 per cent discount. Thus, if a ten-year option is granted to an employee to buy stock at $85 a share at a time when the market value of the stock is $100, and is exercised at a time when the value has risen to $150, and later sold by the employee at $200 a share, only $15 a share is ordinary compensation income. The remaining $100 a share profit is capital gain. In order for a stock option to qualify under the "restricted stock option" rules, the stock acquired under the option may not be disposed of for two years after the option grant, or for six months after the employee acquired the stock through the exercise of the option.

Business men argue that stock options are needed to attract and keep competent executive talent, that the stockholder and the economy benefit because the executives now have a real stake in the company's development and growth. The trouble with these arguments is that the facts of stock option life don't seem to bear them out. Most of the shares optioned to executives of companies listed on the New York Stock Exchange appear to be in the hands of senior executives who wouldn't leave the company anyhow, not the bright up and coming youngsters who need to be attracted. For example, Liggett & Myers Tobacco Company offered over half of its optioned shares to ten executives whose average age was fifty-three and who had been with the company an average of twenty-seven years. In the case of Continental Baking Company, the top nine executives who received over half the stock, averaged sixty years of age and thirty-five years of service. At Procter & Gamble, some 45,000 shares were put into stock options, and Neil McElroy, who became Secretary of Defense, received one-third of the shares. Six officers of U. S. Steel bought 32,000 shares under option; Roger Blough, president of the company, received 12,000 of them. While a good deal of raiding goes on between companies, it's open to serious question whether stock options, as distinguished from salary, position and responsibility are the significant factors in attracting talent. In short, a good deal of skepticism is warranted as to the economic need for tax-preferred stock options to attract and keep new talent in corporations.

Moreover, there are those who hold that the growing use of stock options is a bad corporate practice; that elusive and windfall compensation gets hidden; and that stockholders ought to insist on measurable and defined salary payments that give the corporation tax deductions. For stock options deprive the paying corporation of tax deductions for their value. And the compensation windfalls run into large figures. The incentive and business need arguments smack of a rationalization offered to protect a privileged group in a highly profitable tax preference.

Proxy statements required by the Securities and Exchange Commission provide us with all sorts of illuminating insights into how corporations operate. A 1962 proxy statement issued by IBM discloses that in 1956 and 1961 the corporation granted 197 executives options to buy some 265,000 shares of stock; they were given the right to exercise the options over a ten-year period at the market prices when the options were issued. That's quite a deal—a ten-year free play on the market in IBM stock. The nineteen top officers got over a third of the rights—options to buy some 92,000 shares. We don't yet know much about the experience with the 1961 options, but as to the 1956 options, much has happened. Thomas J. Watson, Jr., Chairman of the Board of IBM, received an option in 1956 to buy 11,464 shares of IBM stock at $91.80. By 1962, he had exercised 5,732 of these option rights. Since the stock was selling at $573.75 when the proxy statement was issued in March, 1962, Mr. Watson had a profit on the shares thus bought of over $2,750,000, and despite the collapse of IBM stock with the market break of the spring of 1962, Mr. Watson's indicated profit was still about $1,700,000 at the end of 1962. And he still had 5,732 of the 1956 option shares that he could buy up to 1966 for $91.80 a share. At the end of 1962, IBM stock was selling for about $390 a share; thus Watson had an indicated profit of another $1,700,000, or a total appreciation on the 1956 option of $3,400,000. Economically, this is compensation for Watson's services; most people cannot escape paying ordinary income tax on compensation for personal services. This beneficiary of the stock option special privilege will pay no more than a 25 per cent tax on his profits, so that his additional $3,400,000 of compensation will leave him after taxes with over $2,500,000.

An SEC report for the single month of February, 1961 showed that $123 million worth of shares were bought under stock options by officers and directors of various listed corporations; 350 large companies gave their executives stock-option benefits totalling $200 million in 1959 and $164 million in 1960. A study of these 350 companies discloses that 215 top executives received stock-option benefits (in increases in the value of the stock subject to option) averaging $30,000 in 1960, almost 30 per cent of their salaries; 25 per cent of these executives received stock-option benefits equal to one-half or more of their salaries. And during the years 1959–1960, fifteen of the executives of these companies exercised stock options at prices ranging from one to three million dollars below their then market prices, without tax; and most of this income will produce only capital gain on sale.

No wonder authors who write best sellers, the Hollywood and TV stars and the Elvis Presleys and Chubby Checkers and Mickey Mantles have a right to complain bitterly about the unfairness of the tax laws!

There is a related attraction to highly paid corporate executives in pension plans, which likewise may produce only a capital gains tax. Pensions provided by company contributions are not taxed year by year as the company puts funds into the pension plan. The pension is taxed to the employee only when he is paid his pension, normally after retirement. To a retired executive in a high tax bracket, with income from securities, real estate and other sources, a substantial pension could mean high taxes. Congress once again showed its compassion for the corporate executive and opened another leak in the tax structure by allowing pensioners the benefit of the preferential capital gain treatment, if the executive receives the full amount of his total pension in the single year of retirement. And the same holds true in case of his death, where there's a lump-sum distribution to his beneficiary. Company plans drawn under the direction of corporate executives have accommodated their pensions so as to provide the lump-sum distribution flexibility.

It is to be observed that a company pension plan that gives top management the right to receive a lump-sum distribution and hence a capital gain, will give the same privilege to every other covered employee down to the lowest-paid clerk. Incidentally, that is so largely because Congress, in adopting the tax-pension provisions, required that employers could not discriminate in favor of higher paid employees or management. Indeed, the provisions in the tax law requiring broad coverage and prohibiting discrimination have been a highly important factor in the broad development of comprehensive company-wide pensions. Here the tax law has forced many companies which might otherwise have limited their pension plans to executive and supervisory staff to cover large groups of workers down the line. However, as for the average employee's equal right to lump-sum distributions and capital gains treatment of pensions, the situation is a good deal like the hoary quip about sleeping on park benches—rich and poor alike are free to enjoy such accommodations. Only a tiny fraction of pensioners, those well up the ladder of income brackets, could possibly benefit from capital gains treatment of lump-sum payments.

In 1963, President Kennedy called for an ending of the capital gain preference for stock options and lump-sum pension plan distributions. Under this plan, the spread between market price and the option exercise price would be ordinary income, as would be lump-sum pension plan distributions. The tax would be eased by a spreading provision. The President's recommendation would not, however, interfere with the capital gain treatment under options already outstanding but only with options to be issued. Similarly, ordinary income treatment would not apply to pension plan distributions due to accumulations of credits in a plan built up before this proposal was made.

To qualify for the favored capital gains treatment, we must be selling or exchanging a "capital asset" or a business depreciable asset. Stocks, bonds, inventions, as we have already seen, are capital assets in the hands of the investor and inventor, a sale of which produces capital gain, whereas sales of stock in trade, or books or plays disposed of by the authors produce ordinary income at the full progressive rates. If a Ford dealer sells a car for $2,500 and receives his customer's notes, or a psychoanalyst sees a patient four times and is owed $100, and the automobile dealer sells the notes or the psychoanalyst assigns the claim to a bank, the parties are not selling "capital assets"; consequently, the proceeds are not capital gain but ordinary income. But if the auto dealer sells his franchise to handle Fords or the psychiatrist sells his couch, the profit is taxed as capital gain. These are capital or depreciable assets.

A farmer who sells cut wheat has ordinary income, but a lumberman who cuts and sells timber may have a capital gain. In the privileged area of oil and mineral properties, many recipients of oil, coal and other royalties are treated as receiving capital gains, whereas most other royalties are ordinary income.

If you have never before sold a piece of real estate, you are an investor and may dispose of it on a capital gains basis; but if you have sold three or four parcels within recent periods, you are likely to be a dealer and realize ordinary income—that is, unless you are dealing with one subdivision, in which event perhaps you may sell hundreds of lots on a capital gains basis because it's all part of one subdivision.

And there is an endless myriad of controversies as to where to draw the magic line between capital and non-capital assets. A motion picture was made of the life of Glenn Miller, the band leader. Miller's widow was paid some $400,000 for permission to make the picture; else the motion picture company might have been sued for invasion of privacy. The Government treated the payment as ordinary income. Mrs. Miller went to court to sustain her claim that she had given up a property right in the story of her husband's life and so had sold a capital asset; the court agreed with the Government.

Francis, the talking mule, a character created by a "lonely second lieutenant in the Pacific theatre of operations, who sometimes wondered whether there was anything lower in the army than a second lieutenant," produced an amusing case in drawing the lines between ordinary income and capital gain. When the creator of Francis sold his Francis novels to Hollywood, he also sold all his rights in the character, Francis. With a refinement of distinction that only Jesuits or Talmudists are likely to appreciate, the author's lawyer argued that what the author got for the novels on the sale was ordinary income; but that what he got for the character Francis produced capital gain. And that was because Francis was not a "literary property" but was instead an "intellectual conception"! The court concluded that however you looked at Francis, he was a "literary composition," the sale of which produced ordinary income.

I could go on page after page citing literally hundreds of cases that have arisen as to how to draw the tortuous line between assets that qualify for capital gain treatment and those that do not. It is one of the most vexatious and slippery technical problems in the income tax field. While plausible explanations can be offered for virtually every nice distinction drawn, as a matter of equality between tax-payers, the whole complicated structure is indefensible. Investors selling stocks or real estate, corporate executives benefiting from stock options and pension plans, oil and timber men, and more recently inventors, have become preferred members of our society, enjoying the advantages of capital gains taxation, while most taxpayers are subjected to the progressive, ordinary income schedule, and in consequence carry part of the load the favored classes ought to bear.

Capital gains are concentrated in higher income levels. For 1959, 4.6 million individual tax returns reported sales of long-term capital assets, with net long-term gains of $12.3 billion. Somewhat over 40 per cent of the total net profits arose from sales of stocks and 20 per cent from real-estate transactions. While more than 3 million individuals with incomes under $10,000 reported capital gains, their profits averaged only about $1,000 per return. At the top of the income pyramid, 266 returns filed by persons with incomes of $1 million or more showed an average of $2 million of capital gains. Or looked at from the point of view of returns with incomes over $50,000, the 1959 figures disclose that the 3 per cent of our taxpayers in the highest brackets received 36 per cent of the $12.3 billion of the total net long-term gains reported. If the treatment of capital gains in our law is justifiable, the justification must be found in some overriding economic considerations; else these inequalities in tax treatment are a subversion of our income-tax system. And there are many who hold that the maintenance of a free flow of investment funds into our productive system fully warrants these differences in tax treatment.

We shall shortly turn to a discussion of the economic considerations offered in support of the preferential treatment of capital gains. But before doing so, we must fill in one more link in the chain of capital-gains taxation—the death escape hatch for untaxed capital gains. We do not tax profits on the sale of property until they are realized. If you had bought 100 shares of General Motors common stock at the end of 1947 at the then market price, you would have paid about $5,800; and if you still held it fifteen years later, at the end of 1962 the stock would have then been worth some $36,000. Or if you had bought 100 shares of General Electric stock at the 1947 date, you would have paid approximately $3,600, while fifteen years later if you still held it, the shares would have had a value of $23,000. You would not have paid any tax on the appreciation. That's because we do not tax the appreciation year by year; we tax the appreciation only when you sell or exchange the asset, and then at preferential rates.

There are economists who hold that the only correct way to treat capital gains is to tax any increase in value (and allow a deduction for any decrease) year by year, regardless of whether you've sold; and that the increase ought to be taxed as ordinary income, and the decrease allowed as a deduction. However, this theoretical position has never commended itself to tax administrators, who shudder at the virtually impossible job of valuing annually every stock and bond, every piece of real estate, all businesses and every other capital asset in the land.

Nor has Congress been willing to force people to pay income taxes on appreciation that has not been converted by sale into cash or notes or other assets; people need cash with which to pay taxes. Consequently, the theoretical ideal of taxing annual unrealized appreciation has had to yield to the practical facts of life, with the consequence that unrealized gains are not taxed.

We have carried this principle to the point where we do not tax unrealized appreciation even when a man dies. Thereby hangs the tale of one of the most severely criticized provisions in our tax law, that at a man's death unrealized appreciation in his assets is not taxed. His heirs acquire a new tax cost (tax basis) for the assets, a cost measured by the value of the property on the date of the owner's death (or at the estate's option one year later). This means then, to take the General Motors or General Electric cases mentioned earlier, that the approximately $30,000 in appreciation in GM stock since 1947, and the $19,400 rise in the General Electric stock, *will never be subjected to income tax*. The decedent never paid an income tax on this increase in wealth because he never sold or exchanged it. His death is not a taxable disposition for income tax purposes, and his heirs or beneficiaries have a tax basis, by which their profit on a future sale will be measured, equal to the stock's value on the date of death. The appreciation thus escapes income tax altogether, although it is included in determining estate tax.

The magnitude of the problem of untaxed gains is seldom appreciated. There is more unrealized gain not taxed than realized gain that is taxed! Thus as of December, 1960, the New York Stock Exchange estimated that there was $100 billion of appreciation in the $250 billion of estimated stocks held by individuals in this country, 40 per cent of their value. For 1960 total net long-term capital gains of $11.7 billion were reported in income-tax returns, a drop from the $12.3 billion for the peak year 1959. As Professor Harold M. Groves, a leading tax economist, has put it, "capital gains are like an iceberg with the larger part below the surface constituting gains that are never officially realized." In any reform of the capital-gains tax, the elimination of the capital-gains death escape hatch is a must. In 1963, President Kennedy urged Congress to do so as part of his tax reform package. But up to now, this glaring deficiency in the income tax structure is a good deal like the weather—

everybody talks about it, but Congress does nothing about it.

If the lower rate of taxation of capital gains is warranted, the justification must be found in the economics of the investment market and the compelling need to provide a tax incentive to a constant flow of capital into investments. There is a strong body of opinion that argues, often with passion, that the overriding investment needs of our economy not only warrant but compel the continuation, and indeed, the greater liberalization of the existing preferential tax treatment of capital gains.

The New York Stock Exchange and other spokesmen for the financial community advocate the elimination of all tax on capital gains, or if that cannot be accomplished, a cut in the maximum capital-gain rate to 12½ per cent and a three-month holding period, instead of the present six months requirement for long-term gains. They point out that billions of dollars of capital gains are "locked in" by the capital gains tax; that investors are not free to sell and reinvest in other ventures because of the capital gains tax. A recent study made by the Exchange, based on questions put to investors, concludes that if the maximum tax on capital gains were cut from 25 per cent to 12½ per cent, investors would "free" $78 billion of this locked-in capital. This locked-in fund is regarded as a tremendous potential for capital formation, for meeting the billions of dollars of new equity capital and other financial needs of the economy. The capital-gains levy is characterized as a "transfer tax," which, it is charged, "either completely immobilizes or . . . excessively erodes our reservoirs of capital wealth."

Because of our natural propensity for identifying our own economic interests with the public good, we might be inclined to regard with a good deal of skepticism the dire predictions of Wall Street partisans as to the effects on the nation of equalizing the income tax on capital gains and other income. However, the positions taken by the professional investment community are shared at least in part by disinterested scholars. To start with, a study by a group of Harvard economists pointed out that the people who really count in the flow of income into investments are the upper income and wealthy classes. And that's understandable, since about 75 per cent of all marketable stock owned by private investors is held by about 1 per cent of the population—the high bracket taxpayers representing family spending units with incomes above $15,000. This group is interested not in dividends, which are taxed at high rates, but in capital appreciation that they can realize on at the low capital-gain rates. The Harvard study found that the preferential capital gain has caused this investor group to shift funds out of conservative investments and into more venturesome types of investment, such as relatively speculative, marketable common stocks, closely held companies, new ventures, real estate and oil properties. Professor Butters, a member of the Harvard group, concluded that so long as the tax rates on ordinary income are continued at current levels (these were the rates in force in 1962) and men of wealth can put their funds into safe tax-exempt bonds, "any substantial tightening up of capital gains tax would go a long way towards curtailing the willingness of upper-bracket individuals to make venturesome investments."

A somewhat similar position has been taken by Professor Dan Throop Smith of the Harvard Graduate School of Business Administration, who departs from the views of the Stock Exchange as to the type of investments that deserve preferential tax treatment. Thus, he would grant the most favorable tax treatment to long-term investments, those held for at least five to ten years, with intermediate tax rates for holdings of intermediate lengths of time. But he nevertheless holds that there "is probably no single change in the tax law that would do as much damage as an appreciable increase in the tax on true long-term capital gains. An increase would do incalculable harm."

A body of opinion has also grown up in this country which favors what is known as the "roll-over" principle of capital-gains taxation. It starts from the view that any capital-gains tax is a serious deterrent to our economic system, and that it is desirable to permit realization on investments, unencumbered by any tax, provided the funds are reinvested. The proposal is that if you "roll-over" from one investment to another, no tax should be paid. The tax would be paid only when you sell the stock and do not reinvest. In this way, investment and reinvestment would be encouraged and the withdrawal of capital from the securities market would be discouraged.

All this reflects one general point of view. Alas, for the bewildered layman looking for certainty and neat answers, the doctors disagree, as they do on most important issues. There is sharp controversy among economists as to the economic effects of the existing capital-gains tax and the elimination of the spread between the taxation of capital gains and other income. The "lock-in" effect of the capital-gains tax is seriously overrated, in the eyes of Professor Walter W. Heller, Chairman of the President's Council of Economic Advisers. To start with, he points out that the major effect of the tax is simply to require people to hold stocks for at least six months; that the rational investor wants to buy low and sell high, and that "the sophisticated investor doesn't allow the tax collector to make his market decision." Moreover, Dr.

Heller contends that the capital-gains tax cannot be much of a deterrent to shifting investments, because if the new investment is attractive on its own merits, a comparatively slight increase in income or in the value of the new investment will offset the tax. Besides, nearly 20 per cent of all listed stocks are held by institutional investors, banks, insurance companies, mutual funds, universities, and tax-exempt pension plans which are in the business of investing funds and are becoming an increasingly important factor in the investment market; and they are not likely to be much affected by the existence of a capital-gains tax.

The deterrent to new investments through a capital-gains tax that would more closely approximate the tax on regular income is far from being demonstrated. Established businesses largely finance their expansion through their own retained earnings, the part of their profits that they do not pay out to their stockholders (about which we shall have more to say later). Professor Harold M. Groves told a Congressional Committee in 1959, "As the late Henry Simons [author of a classic study of the income tax] was wont to insist, it seems very doubtful that the progress and success of our free-enterprise system has very much at stake in the tax favors granted to capital gains."

While it is important, in order to induce people to invest funds in businesses, that a ready market for sales of securities be maintained, the tremendous daily turnover in stocks (five million shares on an average day on the New York and American Stock Exchanges, with over 1¼ billion shares sold in 1962) adds not an iota of capital to any business. These are to a large extent speculative transactions by persons who provide no new funds for any business, but transfer funds from one stockholder to another. The vast number of speculative transactions appears to be beyond all proportion to what is required to maintain a reasonable market for true investors. If a more stringent capital-gains tax reduced the enormous volume of short-term trading by speculators, it might be that no real hurt would be suffered in terms of the flow of funds into businesses, new and old. As a University of Pittsburgh economist, Raymond L. Richman, has pointed out, "the purchase of outstanding securities is not investment from the social point of view. . . . In the interest of economic growth, one would like to encourage investment in capital goods, capital formation. . . . It would seem that the privilege of favorable tax treatment should be restricted to those making the original investment in capital goods; and dissavings by security holders discouraged by treating capital gains in all other cases as any other kind of personal income. Economic growth would be stimulated, and the 'fast-buck' and 'easy-buck' stock market fever abated."

There is another factor to be noted. In our great push to encourage investments, we may be ignoring the fact that there may be limits to the amount of the investment that is good for the economy; for productive capacity may outstrip our capacity to consume. And the pattern of investment that is stimulated by the sharp rate differentials between ordinary income and capital gains may frequently be hurtful to the economy. We may be pulling investment capital from the reasonable needs of the economy to foolhardy and risky ventures, dictated by hope of capital gain with its tax benefits.

Finally, there is the great debate epitomized by Professor John K. Galbraith's *The Affluent Society* as to whether too much of our national product does not already go into providing goods for private consumption. There is a respectable school of thought that contends that more of our economic output ought to go into the public sector of our economy, that our prime need is not for more two and three-car families, bigger and better tail-fins, or more speed boats and mink coats, but for more schools and scholarships, more low and middle-income housing, better paid teachers and social workers, and other public services and facilities. If our emphasis needs to be shifted to expanding the public sector of our economy, the great mobility and easy liquidity of private capital through preferential tax rates may be of less importance than in an earlier era of the development of industry. And the collection of higher taxes from sales of securities and other capital assets may help provide badly needed revenues for such public use of funds.

What conclusions can the searching layman draw from this welter of conflicting views and differing judgments of economists as to the impact of a capital-gains tax on our economy? The answer to this dilemma is not a simple one, for taxes, like life generally, are full of compromises. Would that we had a divining rod for finding the right spot at which to yield on this or that principle to an overriding social or economic need! Wise tax statesmanship does require that equity and equality of treatment give way to the sensitive dynamics that power our economy. Thus, the broad tax exemption granted to new businesses by Puerto Rico in its Operation Bootstrap produced tax bonanzas to certain businesses and was by its nature discriminatory and preferential. But from all reports, these tax incentives have boomed the Puerto Rican economy, brought badly needed new ventures, and helped build up employment and the standard of living in Puerto Rico, to the benefit of the community at large. It may be that the investment credit for new investment in machinery and equipment recommended by the Kennedy administration and adopted by Congress in 1962 is likewise a desirable piece of tax legislation. This credit gives a preferential cut in tax rates to businesses that add new machinery and equipment, but not to service enterprises, and it gives little benefit to those that do not use large amounts of machinery and equipment. It is designed to produce new jobs and relieve unemployment. In short, it is at times wise statesmanship to grant preferences and special advantages as a price worth paying for the larger good of the whole society.

Nevertheless, we ought to exercise the utmost caution in compromising the principle of tax neutrality in response to pleas that tax preferences are required by the needs of the economy. Every group in the country—manufacturers, oil companies, labor unions, universities, insurance companies, cooperatives, airlines and Broadway restaurants alike—seems capable of persuading itself that the welfare of the nation requires that *it* be granted preferential tax treatment. And there always seem to be learned economists, sundry university professors and sophisticated tax lawyers ready to document the case for any group. The classic words of Charles Wilson, then President of General Motors, that "what's good for General Motors is good for the country," will find their echo in every nook and cranny of our community. Just talk to almost any stock broker and you will learn that our capitalist system cannot survive unless all taxes on capital gains are repealed; and if you seem receptive, he is likely to load you down with literature to support his view. Or spend half an hour with an officer of an oil company, and you will learn that if percentage depletion on oil wells is repealed, we shall lose the cold war to communism.

We need to maintain a good healthy skepticism in listening to pleas for tax preferences. The United States Treasury has been plundered too often by vested interests seeking, with spurious arguments, unwarranted preferences in the name of the needs of the country. It's very easy to be deluded in this area, for we are dealing with controversial economic problems, which cut into basic philosophies and deep-seated predilections. Actually, the facts as to the economic effects of this or that tax change are frequently speculation and unverifiable guesswork.

As a matter of equity, few would deny that capital gains deserve the same treatment as other income. Likewise, if we are to tax capital gains in the same way as salary or interest or other income, it is agreed that we must do something about the "bunching" problem. It would be unfair to pile up the appreciation over a period of years and tax it all at high-bracket rates as if earned in the year of sale. This problem can, however, be solved through an averaging device. The profit would be spread evenly over the years the stock was held. This is a technique that we are familiar with and now use in other branches of the tax law. Thus, if a lawyer receives in a single year his entire fee for work done over a period of thirty-six months or more, we permit him to spread it evenly over the period he worked on the matter. We could apply a similar technique to capital gains. Consequently, we do not need so crude an instrument as a flat 25 or 19.5 per cent tax, or taxation of only half the profit at ordinary rates to deal with the appreciation over a period of time. True, spreading would add a complication to those who choose to spread their income; but such a complication is decidedly preferable to the low rates of tax for the investor now in force.

Given the importance of investment in our economy, particularly in untried and newer ventures, there are few economists who are willing to go so far as to recommend complete elimination of the differential between ordinary income and capital-gain rates, at least so long as our present individual rates remain as high as they are. Nevertheless, in the reconciliation of the competing interests of equality among taxpayers and the nation's need for a steady stream of new capital investment, a substantial narrowing of the gap between the capital-gains rates and the ordinary income rates has much to commend it. If Congress should adopt the Administration's proposal to reduce rates and cut the top individual rate from 91 to 65 per cent, the reduction of the capital-gain rate to 19.5 per cent, as proposed, would, I suggest, move us in the wrong direction. Instead, I would urge that the top capital-gain rate be *increased* to perhaps 35 or 40 per cent (with a corresponding adjustment in the amount of capital gain taxed, if the alternative capital-gain rate is not used). Such a plan would go part of the way in reducing the preferential treatment of the investor under the income tax law, and at the same time retain some of the tax advantages needed to encourage investment.

What is to be said of the roll-over proposal? So long as a taxpayer is in the stock market (or perhaps in real estate), he could buy and sell and move from one investment to another without tax. The rest of us get no such boon; we pay tax on salaries and savings-bank interest, royalties and fees, as we go along. The roll-over idea would tremendously widen the inequality already existing between investors and the rest of the community. Indeed, investors would have Uncle Sam's money to speculate with; for if a $100,000 profit is made on a sale of securities and no tax is payable because the profits are reinvested in other securities, the taxpayer is using $25,000 that would otherwise go into the Treasury for investment purposes. And if investors were to invest and reinvest over a lifetime, huge sums, that would in effect be interest-free loans from the Treasury, would be available for reinvestment. Such pressure for reinvestment—few would want to hold funds uninvested if reinvestment would avoid the tax—could produce highly speculative and uneconomic stock-market operations. Thus, the roll-over proposal would not only accentuate the favored position of the investor over most other taxpayers, but would also tend to produce economic consequences of dubious social desirability.

If we were to combine the roll-over proposal with the escape of income tax on untaxed appreciation on the death of the security holder, the tax-free cycle would be complete. No income tax would ever have been paid on the stocks or bonds or other eligible assets bought and sold during the holder's lifetime, so long as the funds were reinvested in similar property. This result would be indefensible and, indeed, the advocates of the roll-over principle usually recognize this weakness in the tax structure and couple their plan with one technique or another for taxation of untaxed appreciation at the death of the owner. Nevertheless, regardless of this feature of the plan, the roll-over proposal is one that moves us in the wrong direction—more tax privileges, more avoidance of tax for the security holder, while others foot the bill. It would require an overwhelming case of economic necessity to adopt this proposal. The case made out to date does not warrant opening such a new hole in the tax structure.

Turning to a different segment of our economy, it might be desirable to use preferential capital-gains treatment to aid smaller business. The financing difficulties of the small business in our economy are frequently insuperable. We have used Government aid, through loans, to keep, main-

tain and strengthen small businesses; and we have adopted
some preferential tax measures to encourage investment in
small businesses. Examples of such measures are the allowance of an ordinary loss (instead of the limited capital loss)
to an investor in a Small Business Investment Corporation,
the special allowance of up to $20,000 in additional de-
preciation for the year new equipment is bought, and the
election granted to certain corporations to be taxed more or
less like partnerships. We could allow more favorable tax
treatment to profits or losses, on the disposition of investments in small ventures, as a means of encouraging such
investments, at the same time as we cut back on preferential
tax advantages for investments in larger businesses.

If we are to retain some preferential advantages for the
investor in businesses, large or small, we ought to confine
the proposal and safeguard its reach so as to be responsive to
the market reasons for adopting it at all. At the outset,
only an *investor* ought to be covered by the capital-gain
provision, not an inventor or an author or an unincorporated
actor (this matter is discussed in Chapter 5). This is not
because we love men of money and look down on creative
talent or professional services. It is only because of the belief that the preferential tax advantage to the investor is
important to the accomplishment of economic goals that
transcend in importance this inequality in taxation. Consequently, we ought to outlaw capital-gains treatment for
persons in service industries, and for noncapital investments, because the compelling economic necessity warrant-
ing tax inequality does not exist in these areas.

Likewise, investments ought to be limited to dedication
of capital to a business for a substantial period; certainly
far longer than six months, or a year as proposed by the
Treasury in 1963, which are periods designed to reward

speculators, not investors. A holding period of a minimum of perhaps two or three years ought to be required to qualify for capital-gains treatment.

Certainly, the death escape hatch needs to be closed up, coupled with a provision for averaging the tax on gains over some reasonable period, and allowing the estate or heirs time to sell the assets to raise funds for tax payments.

Finally, much can be done in the technical circumscription of what goes into the capital-gains pot to eliminate abuse. Pension lump-sum payments, stock options, coal and timber royalties—all these and other perversions of the capital gain should be ended; these items should be taxed as ordinary income. These are technical changes, but if "Barkus is willin'," they can be of great importance in cutting down the present broad sweep of the capital-gains preference to the limits justified by the reasons for such treatment.

Over-all, some such changes in the taxation of capital gains are of momentous importance. Without them, it's hard to see how we can go very far in effecting essential equality among taxpayers with like amounts of income.

CHAPTER 4

Taxation of Large Business Enterprises

In our Federal income-tax structure, corporations are taxed as separate legal personalities and their stockholders are taxed on dividends they receive from the corporation. This double taxation of the earnings of corporations, once to the corporate entity and again to stockholders, is unique in the tax law. The business income of individuals and partnerships is taxed only to the owners of the enterprise; there is no income tax on business enterprises, as such, in our tax law. Likewise, wages, royalties, interest and rents are taxed but once.

There is widespread demand for an elimination or at least a softening of the double tax on corporate profits. This is back of the exemption from tax of the first $50 of dividends and a reduction of the tax rate on dividends by 4 percentage points below the taxpayer's usual rate. Should we go the whole hog and eliminate the double tax on corporate profits, by either repealing the corporate tax or freeing all dividends from tax?

The corporate income tax is the runner-up to the personal income tax as a revenue producer. In 1962, it accounted for $21.3 billion, as compared with $50.6 billion for the individual income tax.

The first thing that strikes one in looking at the corporation tax is the enormous concentration of corporate income in a tiny fraction of American corporations. For 1959, the last year for which we have the data (actually the data are for accounting periods ended during July 1959 to June 1960), there were 1,074,000 corporate income tax returns filed. To start with, only 670,000 of these returns reflected *any taxable income*, while the remaining 404,000, nearly 40 per cent of all the corporations, reported deficits. And of those in the black, about 75 per cent had incomes under $20,000. At the summit of the income-tax pyramid, there were approximately 600 giant corporations with net incomes of $10 million or more, which accounted for about $26 billion of corporate net income, over half the net income of all the corporations in the country. Taking the corporations in the $1 million or more net-income classes, there were about 4,500 such companies, fewer than 1 per cent of the corporations with net incomes, and they accounted for about $7 out of every $10 of corporate income. And these 4,500 companies owned some $600 billion, or nearly two-thirds, of the book assets reported by all American corporations showing net incomes.

In looking at these figures, it is important to observe that a large proportion of the small corporations pay no corporate tax at all, because, as individually or closely held and operated businesses, virtually all the corporation's taxable income is taken out as salaries by the officer-stockholders. In figuring taxable income of a corporation, a deduction is allowed for "reasonable" salaries (dividends are not deductible). If all the profits are taken out of the business as salaries to the owners, there is no taxable income. The tests of reasonableness of salaries are pretty generous, because ordinarily it is only in flagrant cases of disproportionately high salaries, or cases in which wives or children who do little or no work are put on the corporation's payroll, that the Internal Revenue Service can succeed in treating the salaries as unreasonable. Consequently, for most purposes the typical small corporation is taxed in essentially the same way as an individually owned business or as a partnership. The income is taxed to the owners, year by year as it is earned, without any significant corporate tax. Nevertheless, there are a good many corporations of intermediate size that do pay corporate taxes, although they account for only a small part of the corporate tax collections.

The corporate tax of some $20 billion a year is thus paid principally by the larger businesses that dominate our economic life.

Turning to the other side of the corporation-dividend levies, the 1960 figures show that $9.9 billion in dividends were reported in individual tax returns; about $400 million were exempted under the $50 exclusion. Who in our community received these dividends, and how were they spread among income levels?

The stock exchanges make much of the wide ownership of stocks in American corporations, estimating that seventeen million people in our country owned stocks in corporations in 1962. Yet, 83 per cent of all families in this country own no stock, according to a University of Michigan study. A look at the income classes in which the dividends are concentrated sheds interesting light on the "widespread" ownership of American corporate stocks. About 75 per cent of the dividends reported in 1960 returns, after the $50 exclusion —$7.1 billion out of $9.5 billion—went to the top 9 per cent of the taxpayers reporting incomes of $10,000 or more. And about 50 per cent of all dividends reported, $4.7 billions, were received by the highest bracket groups, with incomes of $25,000 or more, fewer than 1 per cent of the sixty-one million taxpayers.

There is another way of looking at the dividend figures. How big a percentage are they of total incomes at various brackets? Using 1958 figures, dividends are virtually insignificant for income classes under $10,000, for they amounted to less than 1 per cent of the total incomes; at incomes of $10,000–$20,000, dividends were just short of 5 per cent, but in the $20,000–$50,000 bracket, they account for over 11 per cent of the total incomes. In the $50,000–$100,000 range, dividends reach 22 per cent, and at income levels over $50,000, dividends run to from one-third to over half the total incomes.

The figures leave no doubt that the elimination of the tax on corporations would be catastrophic to the Federal Treasury; and that the repeal of the tax on dividends would mean a loss of billions of dollars a year in revenues. The principal beneficiaries of the expunging of either tax would be the largest and most powerful corporations in the country and our most affluent citizens. Moreover, proposals to reduce the double tax on corporations and stockholders make it necessary, as, indeed, does any proposal for substantial reduction in taxes, to face the ever-intruding question: how are we to make up for the lost revenues? If we are to meet our voracious needs for military expenditures and space exploration, if we are to finance traditional governmental functions and meet the ever increasing demands for Federal aid—for housing, road building, schools and colleges, foreign aid and the Alliance for Progress in South and Central America—we cannot eliminate the corporate tax or the tax on dividends, unless we find that there are other sources from which the funds can be more appropriately raised.

Historically, corporation profits were single-taxed under the Federal income-tax law, like other income. When the income tax was adopted in 1913, we had a "normal" individual and corporate tax, as well as a surtax on individuals.

The corporation paid the normal tax on its profits, and dividends were exempt from the normal tax, so that double taxation was avoided. While there was some measure of double taxation of the corporation and its stockholders during World War I, and for some years thereafter, because the normal corporate rate moved ahead of the personal income-tax normal rate, this was not of major significance until 1936 when substantially full double taxation came into the law. And this remained the law until 1954, when Congress took a stop toward relief from double taxation at the stockholder level. The 1954 revision freed from tax up to $50 of dividends received in any year by a taxpayer, $100 in the case of married couples filing joint returns; and it cut the rate on dividends by four percentage points below the rates applied to other incomes.

A good many foreign countries either do not have a double tax on corporate profits and dividends, or have considerably eased the impact. In England, corporate income is taxed only once; the corporation pays the "standard" rate, but the individual stockholder gets a credit against his tax for the standard-rate tax paid by the corporation. Canada allows stockholders a 20 per cent credit against their personal income tax for dividends received, as contrasted with our 4 per cent credit. In some countries, including Finland and New Zealand, dividends are entirely exempt from personal income tax.

The proponents of relief from the double taxation argue that in addition to the strong equitable support for their position, an easing of the corporation-stockholder tax is imperative in order to maintain and expand our economy. An expanding economy, it is contended, is essential to provide the jobs required by our exploding population. In order to maintain and improve our standard of living, we must have a constant flow of capital for new plant and for research and development. The present tax burden on the stockholder and the corporation are a serious deterrent to capital formation and the flow of new investment money into business. And all this is aggravated by the inroads of automation and the increasingly intense competition for domestic and foreign markets by the dynamic countries of the European common market, by Britain, Japan, and by the Soviet Union and other Soviet-orbit countries. Indeed, it is urged that the survival of American capitalism in world trade and in dealing with the Latin American countries, and the rising new nations in Africa and Asia, makes it imperative that the double-tax deterrent to American business growth be eased.

If wise tax policy suggests that there be some amelioration of double taxation, there are several alternative routes that can be taken. One simple way would be to repeal the corporation tax altogether. This would be a neat and simple solution, but it would mean that, apart from the merits of the proposal, undistributed profits of corporations would go entirely untaxed. Billions of dollars of revenues would be lost, and unless a tax on undistributed profits were levied on shareholders, this route taken alone does not afford a practicable way out.

We could attack the problem from the stockholder level, instead of the corporation level; dividends could be made tax-free to stockholders. The existing $50 dividend exemption is based on this approach. This technique suffers from the defect that it would heavily favor high-bracket taxpayers, who would thus in effect substitute a flat-rate corporate tax for individual progressive rates, and then pay only a limited capital gains tax on their profit when they sell their stock.

Another approach that is widely favored would utilize the British method of treating the corporation tax as a kind of withholding payment made for stockholders, which would reduce their own personal income taxes. Under the British system, the "standard" taxes on corporations and individuals are the same. Thus, if we had a 20 per cent corporate tax and a 20 per cent normal tax on all incomes—with graduated surtaxes on higher incomes—a stockholder who receives an $80 dividend would be treated as if he had actually received $100, consisting of the $20 paid by the corporation and the $80 distributed. Then, in figuring his own tax, he would get credit for the $20 paid by the corporation. The existence of our higher corporate tax rates of approximately 50 per cent, and of individual rates that, for 1962, began at 20 per cent complicates the problem, but does not prevent the British method from being adaptable to our rate schedule. The tax on corporate income, using a 50 per cent rate, could be broken up into two components, a 30 per cent tax on corporate profits and a 20 per cent withholding tax, which would be prorated among stockholders and deducted from their individual taxes. This could be coupled with a tax on undistributed profits to bring pressure on corporations to declare their earnings as dividends to stockholders.

Finally, we could go to the partnership method of taxing corporations. We could repeal the corporate tax and tax stockholders on their shares of the corporation's earnings, whether or not they are distributed. All owners of or investors in businesses would be treated alike, regardless of the form of business organization. And corporations would be under great pressure from their stockholders to distribute a larger share of their earnings than is now the practice, so that each stockholder would be in a freer position to determine when and where his share of the corporate profits should be reinvested. About two-thirds of the revenues lost through the repeal of the corporate tax would, it is estimated, be made up through increased taxes on stockholders.

This approach, if adopted, would produce theoretical equality par excellence. But many regard it as no more than a theoretician's dream, for it ignores dynamic and critical forces in our economy and the practical facts of tax life. By forcing distribution of earnings to stockholders, they argue, corporations would be stripped of the reservoir of retained earnings needed to develop and expand businesses. Unless virtually all earnings were distributed, the owners would frequently have no cash with which to pay their taxes. Moreover, the steep rates of tax to shareholders in the higher brackets on their income from corporations would reduce the sources of reinvestment capital because of the tax bite, and make investment less attractive because of the smaller net return after taxes.

As an administrative matter, the task of determining, year by year, the share of taxable income of the shareholders of every corporation in the country would probably be unworkable. Corporate stock structures, with various classes of common and preferred stock, and differing rights in earnings would complicate the task. And no stockholder's income-tax return could be finally audited until the returns of every corporation in which he held shares had been disposed of by the Internal Revenue Service. The shareholder's final net income would depend on the finally audited net income of the corporation. It is no criticism of corporate accountants to point out that there are inevitable adjustments in auditing the tax returns of corporations of any size, in view of the tremendous number of transactions and items involved, and the large areas of uncertainty, controversy, and differences as to all sorts of matters, from valuation of inventory, to the length of time a new machine will last, to the differences between a deductible repair item and a non-deductible improvement in property. These are the economic and administrative considerations that have impelled many students of taxation, persons who regard the partnership mode of taxation for corporations as sound on its merits, to reject this approach.

There is not much doubt that if you look only at the actual tax dollars paid, the double tax on corporations and their stockholders puts a bigger load on most investors in corporate businesses than on individual business men and partnerships. A study of 1950 taxes made by an MIT economist showed that the great bulk of stockholders paid more taxes through the corporate tax and the tax on their dividends than they would have paid had they received their shares of the earnings in unincorporated businesses. Nearly 3.2 million out of the 3.3 million stockholders were thus "overtaxed." Only the 130,000 stockholders in high brackets were "undertaxed." Measured by the amount of corporate profits taxed, a little over 50 per cent of corporate earnings were "overtaxed," and a little under 50 per cent "undertaxed." The line shifts when we move from the number of stockholders to the amount of dividends paid, because higher bracket taxpayers receive most of the dividends.

But a showing that corporate earnings and stockholder dividends bear more tax than earnings of noncorporate business operations does not of itself make out a case either that there is unfair taxation of corporations and stockholders, or that these taxes unduly discourage investment in corporations. Who actually bears the corporation income tax?

When we talk of double taxation of a corporation and its stockholders, and overtaxation of half the earnings of corporations, we are assuming a critical and highly controversial premise—that the corporation bears the corporate income tax. If that tax is instead passed on to consumers in the form of higher prices, then the stockholder is not bearing the burden; the consumer is.

The inquiry as to the incidence of the corporation income tax, as to who really bears the burden of the levy, whether it is shifted to consumers in the form of higher prices, to workers through lower wages, or to suppliers through reduced prices for their products is one of the most troublesome issues in tax economics. The view of economists over the last few decades had been fairly general that the corporate income tax was substantially borne by the corporation and its stockholders; that it was not, generally speaking, passed on to consumers in the form of higher prices, or passed back to the corporation's suppliers of raw materials through lower prices paid, or to its workers through lower wages. But, more recently, there has been a growing belief among economists that most, if not all, of the corporate income tax is shifted to consumers in the form of higher prices.

Perhaps the most persuasive evidence of this shifting of the corporation tax is provided by recent studies showing that, despite the skyrocketing of corporate income taxes during the last thirty-five years, corporations have still had about the same rate of return on their book net worth, *after taxes*. Between 1920 and 1955, corporation income tax rates quadrupled; they rose from 12½ to 52 per cent. Yet, the *after-tax* earnings on book net worth for large manufacturing corporations remained about the same, 12 per cent in

1920 and 13 per cent for 1952 to 1955. For all manufacturing corporations, the 1920 after-tax return was 8 per cent,
and for 1952 to 1955, it was 8½ per cent. The percentage
of profit on sales has dropped as volume has grown and taxes
have risen, but not the return on book net worth after taxes.
Consequently, many students of the subject hold that corporations and their stockholders have not really borne the
burden of the heavily increased corporate taxes, but that it
has been passed on largely to consumers.

This has been possible in part because our price structure
is largely an administered price system; prices are to a great
extent controlled by the comparatively small group of large
corporations that pay most of the corporate income tax.
These "restrained monopolists"— such powers ordinarily are
lodged only in large corporations—have administered market
prices so as to pass on the tax increases to the consumer.

Let me emphasize that this view is by no means unani-
mously shared by economists. Many vehemently deny that
the more or less constant rate of return during the last
three or four decades of burgeoning corporate income-tax
rates shows that the ultimate burden of the levy falls on
John Q. Public, as a consumer. Some suggest that the taxes
were borne out of increased productivity over the years,
through improved machinery and other methods of cutting
costs; and that because of the heavier and heavier tax bite,
investors have been deprived of their proper share of these
benefits. The consequence has been, they assert, that the
corporate-stockholder tax burden has had a deterrent effect
on our economy, by reducing corporate capital formation
and discouraging new investment.

Before trying to draw any conclusions as to how larger
businesses ought to be taxed, we must explore one other key

area that has a vital bearing on the problem—the retained, undistributed earnings of corporations.

Corporations are not ordinarily required by the tax or corporation laws to distribute all their earnings to their stockholders. As a matter of normal corporate practice, they typically retain a substantial part of their earnings for new plant, new products, acquisition of other companies, expansion of products and services, and for other purposes. The retained earnings are not taxed to the shareholders, although the corporations pay tax on their earnings—both those that are distributed as dividends and those that are retained. Corporate retained profits are very large, indeed. From 1946 to 1954, corporations' retained earnings (including depletion allowances) averaged about $9 billion a year and amounted to slightly over 50 per cent of their earnings. Since 1954, as profits have mounted, both dividend payments and retained earnings have risen; at the same time, the percentage of total earnings retained in corporate treasuries has declined. Dividend payments averaged $12.5 billion a year from 1955 to 1960, and nearly $15.5 billion for 1961 and 1962. Retained earnings averaged $9.8 billion for the years 1955 to 1960, and amounted to about 44 per cent of total earnings; $8.3 billion were retained in 1961 and $10.1 billion in 1962, averaging about 37 per cent of total earnings.

Stockholders in large corporations listed on the stock exchanges or sold over-the-counter may readily convert their shares of these earnings into cash at capital-gain rates by selling their stock. The value of the stock will ordinarily reflect the retained cash or the assets into which they have found their way. This ability to transmute into capital gain undistributed earnings which, if paid out, would produce

dividends taxable at individual rates, is a great attraction to
the middle and upper-bracket investor, and may account
for the ready acquiescence by stockholders in the retention
by corporate managers of a generous part of the corporate
profits. There is, also, always the complete escape of income
tax on retained earnings at death; on the death of the stockholder the retained earnings are never caught in the income
tax net. And as we have seen, the bulk of stock ownership is
concentrated in high-bracket stockholders.

Some corporations, with an assist from the law, make it
possible through the device of stock dividends for stockholders to cash in on their share of undistributed earnings
on a capital-gains basis and still hold onto the rest of their
stock. This practice has been growing in recent years. Suppose you owned 100 shares of Greyhound stock. In July,
1962, the company, instead of paying a cash dividend on its
common stock, issued a 5 per cent stock dividend worth
$1.30 per share. On your 100 shares of the company's stock,
you received 5 new shares worth $130. Under the law, the
receipt of the common-stock dividend was not taxable; you
pay tax only when you dispose of the stock. If you sold the
stock received as a dividend, your tax would be limited by
the ceiling on capital gains, even if you would have been
in a 50 or 60 per cent bracket had you received a cash dividend. This rule goes back to a Supreme Court decision of
more than forty years ago, when the court held that stock
dividends are not income and could not be taxed by Congress under the income-tax amendment to the Constitution.
This was a bitterly contested case; four justices dissented
and many constitutional lawyers have criticized the decision.
Congress has since incorporated the stock-dividend rule into
the Internal Revenue Code, so that this device has legislative approval and is used by a good many corporations.

We have a provision in the law designed to deal with flagrant cases of retaining corporate earnings for tax avoidance purposes. There is a special penal tax ($27\frac{1}{2}$ to $37\frac{1}{2}$ per cent) on undistributed earnings of corporations if the Treasury can show that the earnings have been unreasonably accumulated in order to prevent taxation of dividends to stockholders. This is a heavy burden for the Treasury to carry, and it seldom succeeds in imposing the levy except in extreme cases. Moreover, as a practical matter, the provision is inapplicable to large businesses with a variety of products or activities. In 1962, IBM, for example, had earnings (after taxes) of $241 million; it paid cash dividends of $83 million, while its total retained earnings at the end of the year amounted to $665 million. But who is to say, with its investment in research, computer and data systems, foreign operations and what-not, that IBM unreasonably withheld its earnings to avoid tax on its stockholders? Yet, its high-bracket stockholders undisputably saved taxes because of the retained earnings over the years of two-thirds of a billion dollars; and indeed IBM's record of low dividend distributions, at least prior to the stock market fall in the spring of 1962, helped make it one of the outstanding glamor stocks of the financial community.

The retention by corporations of billions of dollars of earnings annually raises questions that transcend tax matters. With the practice of retaining 40 to 50 per cent of a corporation's earnings, stockholders are deprived by their directors, and as a practical matter in many cases by management, of the chance to decide whether to reinvest the earnings in the business. Some students of the subject hold that this is an unfair practice, that each individual stockholder should have an opportunity to decide for himself how to invest his share of the earnings. They argue that the privilege of reinvestment of earnings entrenches "the tyranny of the board of directors." As Leon Henderson once put the matter, "I hope to see the time when more corporation managers will have to submit to the test of the free market certain decisions which they have autocratically determined upon without reference to the stockholders, or even the major owners, of the corporation." If one is concerned about stockholders being "locked into" corporations (a great complaint against the capital-gains tax), retained earnings are the really serious lock-in problem. Why shoudn't AT&T, Standard Oil, General Electric and IBM compete in the market place, not only with other utilities, appliance and electrical-equipment manufacturers, oil companies and computer producers, but also with a myriad of paper and lumber businesses, real estate companies, department stores, airlines, steel companies and so forth seeking investment funds?

Dividend policy may also be distorted by the self-interest of some managements in expansion for its own sake. Management typically no longer owns a substantial share of the larger businesses its manages. Increased size, power and prestige, accompanied by higher salaries, larger pensions, stock options and other emoluments are strong incentives to management to retain earnings, and to expand and branch out into new enterprises, whether or not these steps are truly in the best interest of stockholders.

A tax on undistributed profits would help solve the tax and the reinvestment aspects of the retained-earnings problems at the same time. It would tend to force larger dividend payments, and thus tax the stockholders on their shares of after-tax corporate profits as they are earned, at ordinary rates, not as capital gains. It would give the stockholders, each individually, an opportunity to decide whether to reinvest in the corporation or elsewhere; and it would provide a substantial new pool of investment funds available to various businesses, large and small, on a competitive basis. True, these funds would be reduced by the individual income tax, but there would nevertheless be billions of after-taxed dollars available to corporations to compete for.

For a brief period we did try an undistributed-profits tax. At the close of World War I, Treasury officials called for a surtax on the undistributed profits of corporations but it was not until the middle thirties that Congress enacted such a tax. In 1936, President Franklin D. Roosevelt sent a special message to Congress in which he called for the abolition of the existing differences between the taxation of corporations and their stockholders and the owners of unincorporated businesses, by repealing the corporate income tax and adopting a graduated tax on undistributed profits. The rate to be used would approximate in revenue collections the taxes that would have been collected from stockholders, had the earnings been distributed. The House Ways and Means Committee, in adopting a proposal along these lines, declared that "the greatest defect in our present system of taxation lies in the fact that surtaxes on individuals are avoided by impounding income in corporate surpluses." The Senate, however, rejected this approach and by the time the bill got through Congress, it was a hodgepodge of compromises, which retained the corporate income tax and imposed a 7 to 27 per cent tax on varying percentages of profits that remained undistributed.

This plan satisfied no one. Some of the law's unpopularity was due to its apparently hasty and faulty draftsmanship, but in addition there was a good deal of hostility to the levy because it was enacted under most inauspicious circum-

stances. The Federal government badly needed new revenues, since the Supreme Court had dealt the Roosevelt Administration a severe blow by invalidating the Agricultural
Adjustment Act taxes, and Congress had worsened the government's fiscal position by passing a veterans' bonus over
the President's veto. Consequently, many critics of governmental spending regarded the tax as having been "con-
ceived in sin." In 1938, the rate of tax on undistributed
profits was reduced to 2½ per cent, and in 1939 the tax
was allowed to expire altogether. This brief flirtation with
the undistributed-profits tax offers little illumination as to
the desirability and impact of such a levy in the long run.

Proposals for taxing retained earnings are usually met
with the telling answer that retained earnings are the economy's seed corn, that they are key to the expansion of industry, and that to tax these earnings would cripple the
nation's growth. There is already widespread concern, in
official quarters as well as among business men and economists, that our productive plant is not growing as rapidly as
those of West Germany, England, Japan and the Soviet
bloc countries. To adopt an undistributed-profits tax now or
to tax stockholders on undistributed income, would, it is
contended, dry up the well of funds badly needed for our
growth and, hence, impede critically required expansion.

Let us look more closely at the record. Corporations have
three major sources from which to finance new plants and
other expansion—depreciation (and in the natural-resources
industries, depletion), retained earnings and the issuance of
stocks, bonds and other debt securities for new capital. A
word of explanation as to depreciation allowances is in
order. If a corporation buys machinery at a cost of $100,000
to use in manufacturing shoes, the cost of the machinery is

an expense of doing business. Just as the manufacturer is allowed a deduction from gross income for wages and rent paid, so it is entitled to deduct the cost of the machines in figuring its income. Since the machinery will last a number of years, the manufacturer is not allowed a deduction for the entire cost of the machines in the year of purchase. Instead, the cost must be spread over the life of the machines. Under the simple straight-line method of determining depreciation, if the machinery is likely to last ten years, $10,000 a year would be deducted from gross income for ten years, so that at the end of the life of the machines, the corporation will have expensed against income its total cost of $100,000.

If the $100,000 capital with which to buy the machinery came from the sale of the corporation's stock, at the end of the ten years, the corporation will have built up a fund of $100,000 in its treasury. Its reported profits over the ten years will not have reflected this $100,000, because the depreciation allowance would have reduced its net income by that amount. Consequently, if the corporation had not bought new machinery or if it had used the accumulated depreciation allowances for other purposes, it would have a cash depreciation reserve of $100,000. These funds are now available for the purchase of new plant.

Funds available to businesses for plant and equipment and other purposes through depreciation allowances have grown tremendously in recent years. Partly, of course, this is due to our increased plant; the more depreciable property we have, the larger the depreciation allowances. That is only part of the story; the rest of it lies in accelerated depreciation. Businessmen and their economists have long sought more liberal tax depreciation allowances, and they have met with singular success both from the Eisenhower and the

Kennedy administrations. They have argued that the Internal Revenue Service has given inadequate consideration to obsolescence; that with automation and rapid industrial change, machinery and equipment do not last as long as the Service claimed. Besides, they contended that because machines are most useful and wear out fastest during their earlier years, more depreciation should be allowed during the early life of a machine and be offset by less depreciation during its old age. They buttressed these positions by pointing out that the major Western European countries and Canada and Japan allowed far more rapid depreciation than did the United States Treasury, and that this has worsened the competitive position of American business in world markets.

Why do businessmen press for fast depreciation? If they obtain larger depreciation deductions in the earlier years of their property, won't that be offset by lesser deductions in later years and, consequently, by increased taxes? The great bonanza that lies in accelerated depreciation is that the taxpayer is in effect borrowing money from the Treasury with no interest charge. Take the case of a corporation that would pay $1 million a year in taxes over a ten-year period, using straight-line depreciation. It is allowed to go over to an accelerated depreciation method, which reduces its tax bill for the first five years to $750,000 a year; for the second five years its tax will go up to $1,250,000 a year. While the corporation will still pay a total of $10 million in taxes over the ten-year period, it will have had the use of $250,000 of taxes postponed for a five-year period. Uncle Sam has thus provided the business with working capital, or funds for construction or other purposes, at no interest cost. That is why accelerated depreciation is so rich a business plum.

Moreover, we have assumed a static business that added

no new plant during the ten years. Actually, new plant or equipment would normally be added, so that a new cycle of acceleration sets in each year. Indeed, the experience of American industry, and particularly of larger industry, has been one of continued expansion in recent decades. In those businesses which continue to add new plant and equipment faster than old plant is retired, the tax collector will never catch up with the company!

Accelerated depreciation was recognized in the tax law by Congress in 1954, during the Eisenhower administration. Under the more rapid methods of depreciation thus sanctioned, taxpayers may recover about two-thirds to three-fourths of the cost of the plant and other property during the first half of the life of the property. Depreciation allowances are big chips. As a consequence of the 1954 legislation, annual depreciation allowances *rose* between 1953 and 1960 by $11.2 billion. Of course, normal growth in plant and other depreciable property contributed in part to this rise; but the new depreciation methods were a key factor, for they produced a 60 per cent increase in depreciation rates for 1954–1958 over those used in 1953.

The importance of the mounting depreciation allowances to our immediate problem is that accumulated depreciation, and hence funds available for replacing old equipment and expanding industry, have grown correspondingly. Thus in 1953, American industry (other than financial businesses) spent $23.9 billion on new plant and equipment; its depreciation (and related amortization) allowance for that year was $11.8 billion. In 1961, these industries spent $29.6 billion for new plant and equipment, but in view of accelerated depreciation allowances, they had available $24.8 billion as the year's depreciation (and amortization) allowance. Hence, in 1953 American nonfinancial business had available about one-half the cost of new plant from the year's depreciation and amortization allowance, while in 1961 it could finance over four-fifths of its new plant from the same source. With this large new reservoir of depreciation allowances from which to finance new plant and equipment, the contention of American corporations that they must also withhold from their stockholders $9 billion to $10 billion a year in earnings to replace and expand their plant is seriously weakened.

In 1962, by administrative action, the Kennedy administration gave a still further boost to depreciation allowances by promulgating new depreciation "guide lines," as they are called, which shorten the lives over which machinery, equipment and other property (buildings are excluded) are to be depreciated. This is, of course, a highly technical area in which engineers and mathematicians are having a new field day. But jubilation is in the air in most business circles over the guide lines. Tax men and engineers are pretty generally agreed that the guide lines are a new benefit granted to business, not because the foreshortened lives can be justified by actual experience, but because shorter-than-realistic lives have been adopted to give business a new shot in the arm, in the hope that economic expansion will result.

The Treasury had estimated that the potential increase in depreciation under the new guide lines for all businesses, corporate and noncorporate, based on 1962 assets, would be $4.7 billion a year, an increase of 17 per cent over the depreciation allowable under pre-existing rules. Undoubtedly, this entire amount will not be claimed; thus, a business that has a loss for the year is unlikely to move to the new guide lines. This administrative change was, however, expected to reduce corporate taxes by about $1 billion a year, based on 1962 figures. Here, too, unless business continues to expand, during the older portion of the life cycle of plant and machinery, taxes will rise to offset the then decreased depreciation. However, for the time being, businesses will have additional depreciation reserves for replacement, expansion and growth.

Finally, the 1962 Congress further increased corporate resources by adopting President Kennedy's proposal for a tax credit for new machinery and equipment. Again, to encourage industry to modernize and expand, a 7 per cent credit *against taxes* is given businesses (other than regulated utilities which receive a 3 per cent credit) for new machinery and equipment. The Treasury wanted to limit the credit, in effect, to actual expansion, not normal replacement of equipment, but the 87th Congress was more generous to business and granted the credit for most new machinery, equipment and other depreciable personal property used in business. This provision was expected to cut corporate taxes by about $800 million a year.

Liberalized depreciation guide lines and the investment credit appear to be producing substantially larger tax benefits than the original estimates. A Commerce Department study of 1962 returns disclosed that corporate taxes were cut by $2.3 billion as a result of these administrative and legislative changes in the tax law.

To summarize, American business has mounting new resources with which to meet its requirements for replacement and expansion. In recent years, it has typically been generating enough cash through depreciation allowances and retained earnings to finance plant and equipment for replacement and expansion. Thus, in 1961, these internal sources provided all the country's nonfinancial corporations with $32.1 billion, while $29.6 billion was spent on new plant and equipment; and in 1962, these sources generated $35.3 billion, while $32.3 billion was spent on new plant and equipment. True, American corporations actually spent more money than they obtained from internal sources—inventories were increased, more funds were retained as working capital, and accounts receivable increased. New issues of stocks and bonds were floated to raise $9.6 billion in 1961 and $7.2 billion in 1962. Nevertheless, with liberalized depreciation, guide lines and the investment credit, plus the likelihood that internal corporate resources will continue to grow, the case for enacting some kind of tax measure to prevent the escape of the dividend tax on at least a substantial part of the retained earnings of $9 to $10 billion a year is an impressive one.

Let us retrace our steps. We have found that the corporate tax is essentially a tax on larger corporations, with 70 per cent of it being levied on the fewer than 4,500 corporations with net incomes of over $1 million a year. The dividend tax is largely a levy on incomes of over $10,000 a year, which receive nearly three-fourths of all dividends declared. The repeal of either the corporation tax or the dividend tax would mean serious revenue losses to the Treasury. Neither course is dictated by compelling economic considerations or by the requirements of equity. The internal resources of corporate business and the prospects of even larger resources in the years ahead are of such magnitude that the time appears to have come to enact a tax measure which will force payment out to stockholders, and subject to dividend tax at least a substantial part of the $9 to $10 billion a year of profits retained in corporate treasuries.

Throughout, we have been focusing our attention on the large corporation, leaving the smaller corporation, with its

own characteristics and its peculiar problems, for later consideration. Where should we draw the line between the
larger corporations that would be subject to the corporate
tax and whose stockholders would pay a tax on dividends,
and other corporations? This is a line that needs more extensive examination than can be done in this work; but one
possible line suggests itself from the basic data as to corporate bigness that we have been examining. We could use
size of income or size of book assets, or both, as our yard-
sticks. If we subjected to the corporate-stockholder levy,
corporations with annnal net incomes of $1 million or more
during the taxable year, or perhaps over a period of two or
three years, we would be encompassing the approximately
4,500 corporations that in 1959 accounted for 70 per cent of
corporate income. Or if we applied the tax to corporations
with book assets of $10 million or more, we would be em-
bracing the approximately 7,500 largest corporations in the
land. These standards could afford a basis or bases for drawing the tax line, bases which could be modified or adjusted
in the light of experience.

In considering the technique to be used in dealing with
the retained earnings problem, the proposal that earnings
of the larger corporations be taxed to these stockholders,
whether or not distributed, seems clearly unacceptable. Not
only is this remedy fraught with too many administrative
difficulties and dollar hardships to stockholders to warrant
its adoption, but the evidence is persuasive that we ought
not and cannot afford to give up the double tax on such
corporations and their stockholders. Consequently, what is
required, it would appear, is an undistributed-profits tax,
which is a flexible and workable instrument for achieving
the desired results, and which avoids the possible hardships
to stockholders of paying taxes on dividends they do not

receive. We might, for example, tax the undistributed earnings of larger corporations at a 20 per cent rate, which would mean that distributed earnings would be taxed at about 50 per cent (approximately the current rates), and retained earnings at 70 per cent. Thus, on $1 million of corporate profits, there would be $500,000 available for distribution after a 50 per cent tax. If no part of the $500,000 were distributed, the corporation would pay an additional $100,000 in tax—20 per cent of $500,000. Doubtless we would want, as a margin of safety, to allow some earnings to be retained by all corporations, which could be a fixed dollar sum per year, or perhaps a minimum percentage of profits which could be retained each year without being subjected to the undistributed-profits tax.

Such an undistributed-profits tax, as applied to larger corporations, would exert strong pressure on corporations to distribute their earnings to stockholders, except for the minimum retention that would be permitted without the tax. Stockholders would doubtless demand such distribution, rather than allow the corporation to incur the additional tax. The revenues from taxes on dividends would increase, and the opportunity to convert ordinary income into capital gain would be diminished. Stockholders would become masters of a greater share of corporate profits, to do with as they choose, to spend on consumer goods or for reinvestment, after, of course, Uncle Sam has taken his cut. There would be a larger supply of investment funds available in the open market, once the captive billions of retained earnings were freed, albeit reduced by the tax on dividends. There would be a reinvigorated securities market in which corporations would have to compete with all bidders for the funds. All this would, I suggest, be wholesome and healthy both for the fisc and for the world of corporate finance.

The amount or percentage of earnings that would be permitted to be retained without the special tax, and the rate of the levy, and other aspects of the tax, would be open to re-examination and reconsideration in the light of experience. And we would have to adopt the usual gamut of technical provisions to prevent avoidance of the taxes and provide relief for hardship cases. For example, in determining what is a larger corporation by size of income or assets, we would want to prevent avoidance of the tax by the breaking of a large corporation into many separate or subsidiary corporations; presumably a controlled or related group of companies would be treated as a unit. We would doubtless want special provisions adapted to the peculiar needs of banks, insurance companies and other companies. Likewise, where a corporation had a bond issue outstanding before the tax became law that prohibited its paying out dividends but required their use to pay off the bonds, relief would be in order. These are illustrations of the numerous problems that the technicians would inevitably have to struggle with; but the principle of forcing greater distribution of retained earnings by large corporations through an undistributed-profits tax is, I suggest, the direction in which we ought to move in refashioning the corporate tax as applied to larger enterprises.

A final note as to the entire approach to corporate taxation. We are dealing with economic and fiscal problems about which there are sharp divergences among the experts as to key underlying factual data (such as the incidence of the corporate tax), and as to the impact on our economy of conflicting courses to be adopted. How is the inquiring citizen to formulate his views with respect to such complicated fiscal problems as whether the overriding requirements of our economic system require an easing of the corporation-stockholder levies? How is he to decide whether to cast his ballot for candidates for Congress who support the current corporate tax structure, or for those who are pledged to seek relief from the corporation-stockholder double tax, or for those who advocate an undistributed-profits tax on top of the present levies?

Perhaps the answer lies in your over-all economic philosophy, in your basic views as to what makes our economic system tick. Do you look on the encouragment of the flow of investment capital into business and internal corporate capital formation—that is, the building up of large after-tax reserves in corporate treasuries to finance new plant, new products and new ventures—as the keys to an expanding economy and full employment? Or is the key to our economic welfare to be found at the other end of the economic spectrum, in consumer spending? Is our making available to the consumer a larger amount of income the dynamic essential to the creation of new plant, new products and new ventures that will prove profitable to the investor? In considering the argument of those who hold that if the corporate tax is passed on to consumers, it ought to be repealed in order to relieve consumers of this burden, how much faith do you have that, in our administered price economy, the benefits of an elimination of the corporate tax would be passed on to the consumer through reduced prices? Will the result be instead larger profits to stockholders and new sales taxes on consumers to make up the revenues lost through the easing of taxes on corporations or stockholders?

The question is: what is your economic vantage point— the trickle-down theory or the push-up theory? Or if you recognize that there is merit in both approaches, where do you put the major emphasis? In the final analysis, it is your economic faith, your socio-economic tropism—perhaps un-articulated and ill-defined but nevertheless, like our emotions or our unconscious mind, a powerful influence on our lives—that is likely to determine your alignment with respect to most of the critical, controversial issues of taxation, including the controversy as to whether the double tax on corporations and stockholders should be retained, or ameliorated or abolished altogether. Viewing the facts we have developed from the vantage point of my own economic outlook, I am not persuaded, in the case of large corporate enterprises, that the present basic structure of a corporate income tax and a dividend tax ought to be done away with. Instead, particularly in view of their large internal capital resources, I would retain this essential structure for the large business and seek to strengthen it by the addition of an undistributed-profits tax.

CHAPTER 5

Tax Gimmicks Incorporated

When we turn from the taxation of the large corporations, whose operations spread across the nation and beyond, to the hundreds of thousands of small corporations that are an integral part of our way of life, different problems arise, problems which require their own treatment. We have already observed that the tax law accepts the corporation on its own ground, and treats and taxes it as a separate entity, without taxing its stockholders on retained earnings; and that the stockholder can realize on the earnings retained by the corporation by selling his stock. The consequence is that the stockholder pays only the capital-gains tax on his profit in his stock, including the profit reflected in the undistributed earnings.

Individuals and partnerships, we have noted, are taxed quite differently. They pay tax on their earnings year by year as they earn them; they cannot accumulate them untaxed in the business and then sell them off at the capital-gain rate. This difference between the taxation of individuals or partnerships and corporations lies at the bottom of some of the most elegant tax-avoidance schemes ever devised; and efforts by Congress to put a stop to these devices have produced some of the most complicated provisions of the tax law. Because a knowledgeable approach to the proper taxation of the small corporation requires some understanding of the abuse of the corporation for tax-avoidance purposes, I propose to review some of these tax-avoidance devices and the techniques adopted by Congress to bar their use.

A Congressional investigation into tax avoidance and evasion made in the middle thirties revealed to a shocked public that wealthy taxpayers had incorporated country estates, racing stables, expensive yachts and elaborate town houses. A yacht or country estate or a racing stable was transferred to a corporation, all of whose stock would be held by the owner, along with stocks and bonds or other income-producing assets. Thus, in 1929, Alfred P. Sloan, Jr., President of General Motors, organized a corporation which took over a contract Sloan had made for the building of his yacht. The corporation, all of whose stock Sloan owned, paid over $1 million for the yacht; it obtained the funds by selling stocks Sloan had turned over to it. At the same time, Sloan transferred to the corporation about $3 million of other securities he owned. The income from these securities was used to pay the expenses of operating the yacht, and although Sloan paid his corporation charter fees of about $100,000 a year, it actually cost from $185,000 to $223,000 a year to keep up and operate the yacht. The dividends and other income from the securities were used to pay these additional costs, which were taken as deductions by the corporation as part of its "business" of operating the yacht. By this corporate device, Sloan avoided tax on about $800,000 of income from securities over a seven-year period and saved nearly a quarter of a million dollars in income taxes.

In the same way, incorporated town houses, country estates and racing stables were used to pay the expenses of lavish living for high-bracket taxpayers. One wealthy woman went even further and used her personal holding company, which owned and paid for her country estate, to obtain a tax deduction for the cost of her husband's keep; she put him on the corporation's payroll, which claimed a deduction for his salary, and thus offset her income from securities.

The fabulous salaries of motion-picture stars and directors, and the large royalties paid to authors for the motion picture and TV rights to popular novels gave rise to another device to circumvent personal income tax rates: the incorporated talent. If a motion-picture star is paid $200,000 to make a picture, such income piled up in one year will not provide much after taxes for living in the "grand manner," or to "stash" away for a leaner day. And while it is true that there are devices for spreading the income over a period of years, that would not be of much value to a Bing Crosby or a Danny Kaye, an Elizabeth Taylor or a Bob Hope, whose pictures or TV performances continue year after year.

Such high-bracket taxpayers viewed with intense envy the business man who can do business through a corporation. Why not incorporate talents? True, corporations were created for business ventures, but why can't they be used to accomplish for personal-service income the same benefits that business income receives? As a result, some motion picture and TV stars incorporated their talents by setting up their own corporations, all of whose stock they and their lawyers or agents owned. The star agreed to work for the corporation at a salary much lower than the actual fee to be paid for his services, and the corporation made the contract with the studio or broadcasting company for the star's performances. The corporation received a deduction for the salary paid the actor; the balance of the fee for his services remained in the corporation, taxable at corporate rates, and the corporation was then used as an investment vehicle. If the star needed money, he could borrow from his corporation; and eventually, if desired, the assets of the corporation could be taken out through liquidation at the preferential capital-gain rate. True, this meant an over-all corporate tax and a capital gain, but these combined rates were often significantly lower than the direct individual tax rates on the income.

Congressional investigation into tax avoidance and evasion in 1937 disclosed the case of a radio broadcaster who had a contract with the Texas Company, which paid him $5,000 for each weekly broadcast. He went through an elaborate incorporation set-up, using four corporations; the broadcasting fees were paid to the corporations and the broadcaster received a salary considerably below $5,000 a week. Thereby, the broadcaster sought to cut his taxes for four years by about $200,000. A noted violinist incorporated himself, using two corporations, one for his royalty income and one for his service income and saved some $30,000 in taxes.

Foreign corporations were being formed in the Bahamas, Nassau, Liechtenstein, Newfoundland and other unlikely spots for corporate seats, as tax-avoidance vehicles for holding investments and avoiding tax on personal-service income. The dividends on stocks held by these companies were subject only to a 10 per cent withholding tax, because they were not doing business in the United States; moreover, gains on sales of stocks by these foreign corporations would not be taxable at all. Eventually on liquidation, there would be a capital-gains tax payable by the stockholder, but in the meantime, through loans to the stockholder, the funds could be made available. Hundreds of such companies had been formed in the thirties and there was a great variety of tax-avoidance methods used. One man organized two Canadian corporations, to which he transferred $13 million in securities. Later he borrowed $2 million from these foreign companies (which he owned entirely), paid them $225,000 in interest each year and wiped out all his own taxable income, with the result that he paid no tax. Other persons diverted their patent royalties and commissions for services to their foreign corporations and thereby escaped the usual income taxes. Thus, one actor formed a British corporation which agreed to pay him a salary of $20,000 a year; it received his entire earnings of $190,000 for 1935, which if the plan were to succeed, would sharply cut the actor's tax bill.

Tax-avoidance schemes involving the use of corporations had become so widespread that there was deep concern that it would undermine our income tax system. As Randolph Paul, the distinguished tax lawyer who became President Franklin D. Roosevelt's wartime tax adviser, wrote: "Tax avoidance had developed into a fine art. . . . Something had to be done promptly to save morale, to prevent the income-tax law from becoming a joke, and to offset the imitation-breeding example of successful tax dodging."

President Roosevelt made a strong plea to Congress to plug up these loopholes. "Clever little schemes," said the President, "are not admirable when they undermine the foundations of society." In 1934, Congress had enacted a special tax on the undistributed income of "personal holding companies" to force them to distribute their incomes and thus subject the stockholders to the taxes they sought to avoid. These provisions were strengthened and the rates were sharply increased in 1937. The rate of this penal tax is now 75 per cent on the first $2,000 of undistributed income and 85 per cent on the balance. A provision had also been adopted in 1934 to prevent corporations generally from keeping their unneeded income in the corporate treasuries so as to avoid dividend tax to the stockholders; this is the penalty tax on unreasonable accumulations of income of 27½ to 38½ per cent discussed in an earlier chapter.

"Foreign personal holding companies" were given a drastic treatment of their own, accommodated to the fact that the foreign corporations may not themselves be subject to the American taxing jurisdiction. Instead of trying to tax the corporation, the law taxes the American stockholders on their shares of the income of the foreign personal holding company, whether or not it was distributed. And losses on sales of stocks between a stockholder and his controlled company were disallowed, as were certain types of easily manipulated deductions, such as interest on loans and deductions.

All this was a much needed effort to plug up the more flagrant loopholes in the tax law. And the legislation accomplished a good deal. Up to that point, as one experienced tax lawyer pointed out, tax avoidance was like "taking candy from a baby." Now it became tougher, but the use of the corporation to achieve unwarranted reductions of the tax bills of wealthier taxpayers found new outlets and techniques; new methods were developed to avoid the new law.

I was in the office of a leading New York tax lawyer the day President Roosevelt signed the Revenue Act of 1937, and hailed it as a measure which would put an end to income-tax loopholes. When this seasoned tax practitioner read President Roosevelt's statement, he responded with a loud guffaw. And he, like other members of the tax bar, at once set to work to exercise their ingenuity to circumvent the new law, and with no small measure of success.

Let me mention two or three methods in wide use today, more than twenty-five years later, to circumvent the personal holding-company tax. Suppose a taxpayer has $1 million worth of stocks that throw off $50,000 a year in income. By putting real estate and the stocks into the same corporation, classification as a personal holding company is escaped because corporations over half of whose gross income is from rents are not "personal holding companies." This provision was put into the law for a perfectly good reason; the draftsmen did not want to penalize real estate corporations. Consequently, the 50 per cent gross rental rule was adopted; but this has been successfully seized on by tax men as a convenient device for perpetuating the incorporated investment company.

Or take the incorporated talent. If an actor handles his TV and motion picture performances through a corporation which has substantial holdings in real estate, mineral properties and other enterprises, he too can avoid the penalties of personal holding-company treatment and still route his service income through his corporation. Moreover, many leading and highly paid TV stars are involved in programs requiring a considerable cast of players. Under Internal Revenue Service rules, if an incorporated talent company contracts for the services of the star and all the other members of the cast, only the star's compensation is personal holding-company income; this rule is successfully used to get around the personal holding-company tax for high-bracket TV stars.

Another ingenious device for subverting the normal business functions of corporations for tax purposes, was the more recent development of what became known as the "collapsible corporation." Because *le grand prix* in taxation among the high-bracket élite is the capital gain, the imagination of tax advisers to real estate developers conjured up the notion of *creating* and then *destroying* corporations, as a means of converting ordinary income into capital gain.

A builder of houses has ordinary income when he sells the houses, just as does a manufacturer of TV tubes or men's shirts when he sells his product. How could the builder use the corporation to achieve that modern miracle of alchemy, the transformation of ordinary income into capital gain? The solution found depended on a rather technical provision in the income-tax law, which requires a brief description.

If you own the stock of a corporation and you sell it, ordinarily you have a capital gain on any profit you realize. And the same is true if you sell your stock to the corporation that issued it. Now, suppose instead of selling to your corporation for cash, you sell your stock in the corporation for all its assets. That transaction is dubbed in corporate terminology a "liquidation" of the corporation. Usually, you will have the same tax results on a liquidation as if you had sold the stock for cash to an outsider, a capital gain on your profit. And here's the beauty of the liquidation; the corporation isn't taxable when it swaps its assets with its stockholders for their stock. Out of this pattern of the tax law came the collapsible corporation.

Suppose you and your associates, the builders and the money men, had built, through a corporation, 100 houses on Long Island. They were now ready for sale. You stood to make a profit of $2,500 per house or $250,000, if the deal went well. If the corporation sold the houses, as it normally would have done, there would have been a corporate tax of roughly 50 per cent on the $250,000. Then when you received the remaining cash of $125,000 from the corporation, on liquidation you and the other stockholders would each have paid a further 25 per cent capital-gains tax on the proceeds, or $31,250. This would have left you with $93,750, or a little over one-third of the $250,000 profit. You were not as badly off as if you hadn't used a corporation; but still the tax bite of nearly $2 out of $3 of profit is quite deep.

But by collapsing the corporation, you could have come out with only a total of 25 per cent tax on the profit and have wound up with 75 cents on the dollar, instead of 37½ cents. The way you did it was this: Once the houses were built but before they were sold, the corporation was liquidated, so that the stockholders received the houses in exchange for their stock. When the stockholders received houses worth $250,000 more than their stock had cost them, they had a $250,000 profit; they reported the profit as a capital gain, paying a tax of $62,500. And on the sale of the houses, they paid no tax because their tax cost for the houses was their value when they received them from the corporation.

The collapsible corporation idea was thus a neat twist of the tax law. It spread like a brush fire along the parched Hollywood Hills. Stars, motion picture directors and playwrights enthusiastically embraced the device. The collapsible corporation was tested out in the California Federal District in Los Angeles in a case involving the motion picture production of the Broadway hit play "Kiss and Tell," written by F. Hugh Herbert and produced by George Abbott. When the play opened on Broadway and became a smash hit and Columbia Pictures became interested in doing a motion picture, lawyers and tax specialists were called in and the Abbott-Herbert Corporation was organized. Herbert, Abbott, and their associates in the partnership which had produced the Broadway play became the principal stockholders, and the corporation acquired the motion picture rights to the play. The play was produced on the Columbia lot, with Columbia equipment and technical and other personnel; a bank furnished the money. George Abbott was apparently the executive producer and director of the picture. Columbia distributed the picture through its worldwide distribution facilities. The motion picture was completed in July 1945, and Columbia began to exhibit it. The picture was released in October 1945 and on December 1, 1945, the corporation was liquidated and the legal rights to the motion picture distributed to Herbert, Abbott and the other stockholders. Then, the net receipts of the picture were paid to Herbert and Abbott and the other stockholders by Columbia as they came in, because they now "owned" the corporation's rights in the production. Actually, taxes aside, it appears that they got what they would have gotten had the usual method of licensing the picture to Columbia been used.

In substance, the controversy between Herbert (whose tax case was involved) and the Government, was whether Herbert was entitled to report the proceeds of the picture as a capital gain (technically, the value of his interest in the picture when it was distributed to him), or as ordinary income. The Government argued that the corporation was a sham, set up solely to change ordinary income into capital gain, and that it should be ignored. Herbert won his case and saved about $150,00 in taxes. And presumably, Abbott and the other stockholders likewise succeeded before the Treasury.

Despite the elaborate legal paraphernalia set up, the protestations by Herbert in court that by using a corporation he could retain control of the script of the picture, the testimony of the parties that they had originally intended to set up a going motion-picture business to do a number of pictures (only "Kiss and Tell" was actually produced), one is left with the strong impression from a reading of the case that, in essence, all that was created was a piece of legal legerdemain, having no business function and designed solely to cut taxes. The motion picture's production and distribution were apparently handled about the way they would always be handled. Business went on as usual, on the same studio lots, with the same cameras and sets and the same stars and directors and essentially the same financial arrangements. Only the legal documents changed, now mountainous in volume, incredibly complicated, and understandable if at all only by specialists in motion-picture legal, corporate and tax esotericisms. All this was done with the objective of giving an appearance of reality to a legal setup as unreal as a typical motion-picture melodrama.* But it worked.

By a somewhat similar technique, Pat O'Brien saved himself and his wife a substantial amount of income taxes in

---

* The strange behavior of institutions is illustrated by a curious development that took place in the motion-picture industry. Some tax lawyers insisted that if the corporate set-up were to withstand scrutiny, the actor, director, novelist or dramatist ought to be given some control over the script, the production and perhaps even the budget. The major studios bitterly objected to yielding any such control, but they were prevailed upon— where the stars or directors or writers had sufficient power—to give up some of these controls, often with off-the-record assurances that they were only for Uncle Sam's eyes and not to be exercised.

Also, profit participation deals became more frequent because they helped the tax situation look more like a real business deal, and in some cases, the stars or directors or writers invested small amounts of money or even undertook some financial risks—again to build up the structure against Treasury attack. Out of all this began to come the realization by some of the more influential of the "independents" that they ought to have real control and they ought to share more fully in production policies and in profits. The result was that in some cases a considerable measure of independence did develop and actual business practices began to change. Sometimes free independents did emerge. Hollywood discovered that play acting sometimes boomerangs in real life!

connection with the motion picture "Secret Command."
Jack Benny used a corporation (without a collapsible feature) as a vehicle for the switch of his American Tobacco
Company radio show from NBC to ABC; and the Treasury
failed in its contention that over $2 million of the price
Benny received for the stock of the corporation was compensation for his services. The capital-gain rates were applied to the transaction and Benny saved $236,000 in
income tax.

The increasing use of the corporation created only to die
and through its death to transform ordinary income into
the coveted capital gain, was met with one attack after
another by the Internal Revenue Service, but to a large
extent the Government was rebuffed. It turned to Congress
for relief and the result was the "collapsible corporation"
provision now gracing the tax law. If a corporation is formed
or used principally to manufacture or produce property (or
purchase certain types of property), with a view to selling
its stock or liquidating the corporation before the corporation has realized a substantial part of the income to be
derived from manufacture or production of the property,
then under the present law, the usual capital-gain rule on
the liquidation or sale is barred. Instead, the profit is taxed
as ordinary income.

The statute is complicated and has a number of escape
hatches. If the property is held for three years after production is completed, the collapsible rule doesn't apply. And
the courts have been struggling with what is a "substantial
part of the income to be realized," and at what point the
"evil view" as to the corporation's destiny must come into
play. The Internal Revenue Service holds that at least half
the income must be taxed to the corporation before the

liquidation or stock sale, but the Tax Court has held that one-third is substantial. This means that under the Service's view, one-half the income can come out as a capital gain, and if the Tax Court is right, two-thirds can come out in that guise. Moreover, sales of the films, after they have been "produced" by the "independent" corporations, mergers of "independents" with major motion-picture companies, and other devices being employed may succeed in avoiding or minimizing the strictures of the collapsible-corporation provisions.

The merry whirl between the tapayer and the tax collector continues. Everybody's in a daze except a select group of bleary-eyed tax specialists.

This tale of the abuse and misuse of the corporation, and of Congress' attempts to curb the practices is characteristic of the development of the tax law. A tax-avoidance practice grows up, it is exposed in a Congressional hearing, legislation is adopted to curb it, only to lead to new gimmicks to circumvent the curbing legislation—this is in thumbnail the story of the income-tax law. The result is that tax avoidance gets tougher, tax specialists develop more ulcers as their incomes mount; but a considerable measure of unfairness, inequity and escape from a fair sharing of the tax burden continues.

Now I do not cite weaknesses in the collapsible corporation or personal holding-company provisions to suggest that they are ineffective, or generally speaking, badly drawn. Over-all they are neither, although there are some unfortunate exceptions. Thus, I am inclined to agree with the commentator who characterized the incredibly complicated refinements in the collapsible corporations provisions as a "legislative monstrosity." The result is that the types of tax avoidance dealt with are much more difficult to accomplish than they used to be, and for many they are no longer possible. Nevertheless, for others there are still big gaps in the law.

All this illustrates a key problem in dealing with tax avoidance. Legislation must draw lines; Congress, quite properly, did not want to penalize normal real estate or other operating corporations. The result is that a good many companies that fall within the broad objective of the personal holding-company legislation or the collapsible-corporation provisions are outside their coverage. Of course, if Congress is so minded, as new escapes appear, the law can be changed. Indeed, in 1963, President Kennedy recommended to Congress that the personal holding-company provisions be tightened up to deal with the device of throwing slightly over 20 per cent of non-personal holding company income into incorporated "pocketbooks" or personal-service companies. Under this proposal the 20 per cent rule would be raised to 40 per cent; rents would be counted in figuring this percentage, not in gross but only after deducting interest, real-estate taxes and depreciation; and similar reductions would be made for gross income from interests in oil and gas properties. But the legislative process is a long and difficult one, and there are many vested interests in every tax-saving device, whose political power may bar tax reform.

Also, in plugging each new loophole, there are serious technical difficulties in not covering legitimate business operations which are not intended to be penalized. Inevitably, therefore, few efforts to check tax avoidance can wholly succeed, if we are to do justice to the innocent. A considerable measure of success in preventing the tax-avoidance devices intended to be outlawed is about as much as we can hope for. And that's worth shooting for, as a comparison of the taxation of personal holding companies, foreign personal holding companies, and collapsible corporations at present and before the loophole-closing provisions were adopted, would undoubtedly show. That is as far as we can fairly move, unless more basic and far-reaching reforms are adopted that undercut the entire tax structure. Of that, more later in this work.

This development is also instructive in relation to the widespread and incessant criticism that our laws are too complicated and ought to be simplified. Would it have been preferable, in order to keep the tax laws simple, not to have adopted legislation to close up these loopholes? This is unthinkable, for to do so would have continued to afford easy escape from taxation to some of our highest-bracket citizens. Perhaps, we could have adopted less refined, more sweeping provisions, perhaps some totally different type of solution would have been preferable. But if a penalty provision, like that of the personal holding company is to be adopted, certainly it ought to be carefully circumscribed so as to apply only to the evils to be stamped out, and not to innocent taxpayers not involved in tax manipulation. We here face a dilemma that we shall run into again and again as we proceed with our examination of the income-tax law—to achieve fairness among taxpayers, to close up loopholes without using a blunderbuss that will hurt innocent taxpayers, refinements, complications and elaborate provisions are needed. Simplification of the tax laws is highly desirable and an objective always to be sought; but not at the expense of tolerating flagrant inequities or permitting wholesale escape from tax, nor at the other extreme, of doing unfairness to nonoffending taxpayers through crude and sweeping provisions. This remains a constant and virtually insoluble dilemma of the income tax in a complicated society.

We have been considering a series of tax devices by which the parties deliberately seek to be taxed as corporations. But there is another side to the coin; some enterprises find it advantageous to avoid the corporation tax and be taxed as partnerships or trusts. Moreover, there are large business organizations operating in legal form which are, for all practical purposes, corporations but not, technically, corporate entities. Thus, for many years utility holding companies in Massachusetts operated as "business trusts" that were not corporations because of the peculiarities of Massachusetts law. In some states, real-estate operations are conducted as trusts. In order to subject such entities to the corporate tax, Congress defined "corporations" in the tax law more broadly than incorporated companies. It included within that term all business associations having the essential characteristics of a corporation.

A great deal of litigation has developed over what is an association taxable as a corporation, typically where the taxpayers were trying to avoid the corporate tax. Generally, the classification as an association taxable as a corporation depends upon how freely transferable the ownership interests are; whether management is centralized, as is true in a corporation's board of directors; whether the death of a major owner terminates the venture, as is true with many partnerships but not corporations; and whether the owners avoid personal liability for the debts of the business, a characteristic of corporations and not of most partnerships.

This provision for taxing as corporations unincorporated

associations having the essential characteristics of corporations has produced one of the most bizarre developments in
the entire history of the income-tax law—attempts by members of the ancient and honorable professions to be taxed as
corporations.

During the last two decades, pension plans, Blue Cross,
Blue Shield, health and accident insurance, group life insurance and other employer-financed fringe benefits have
become a standard and important part of the employee
benefit system. These benefits are a thing of beauty in taxation because they are part of the employee's pay package,
but are either not taxable at all (that's true of hospitalization, group medical payments, group insurance) or, as in the
case of pensions, they are not taxable while the employee
is working, but only as he actually receives his pension after
retirement, when his tax bracket has normally fallen. And
these benefits are available to stockholder-executives and
other highly paid corporate employees.

The trouble arose because individual proprietors and partners could not obtain these tax advantages of fringe benefits,
whereas the officer-stockholders of an incorporated business
could. Repeated efforts to have Congress extend these benefits to individual professions and group practitioners failed
(until the passage of the 1962 law that we shall shortly consider). Doctors and lawyers were irked at their inability to
share this tax largesse with the business men and corporate
executives whom they serve.

A group of doctors, or more probably their tax man, con-
ceived the idea of operating through an association taxable
as a corporation. The idea grew up in the obscure town of
Missoula, Montana, where Dr. Arthur Kintner enshrined
his name in the tax men's Hall of Fame by setting up what

has since become known as a Kintner Association. He had been practicing medicine with other doctors in a partnership, a respected and traditional form of carrying on a learned profession. They dissolved their partnership and formed an association for the practice of medicine; the articles of association stated that the organization was to be endowed with "the attributes of a corporation" and that it was to be "treated as a corporation for tax purposes." At least these doctors were frank about why they did what they did, a virtue not always present in tax-avoidance plans.

With a close eye on the court decisions as to what characteristics are needed to qualify as an association taxable as a corporation, the Montana doctors set up an executive committee to direct the work of the association. The doctors became "employees" of the association and received "salaries," while the association collected fees from the patients for the services of the doctor employees. Doubtless, enough salary was paid so that, after rent, help and office expenses, there would be no income left for the association and hence no corporate tax to pay. The key feature of the deal was that a pension plan was set up covering all the "doctor-employees." The formalities of an association were meticulously observed; and we trust the doctors made their hospital calls and served their patients with the same faithfulness as in the past.

The Internal Revenue Service took the position that the practice of medicine involves a personal professional relationship, which cannot be conducted through an association classified as a corporation. But it lost its case in the courts, and Kintner's association was vindicated. The pension plan stood the test.

Yet, all this ran counter to deep-seated tradition and prac-

tice. A corporate medical practice is something of a shocker.
The Hippocratic oath hardly fits a soulless corporation. For
centuries, the professions had been forbidden by law to practice as corporations; for a licensed doctor, not a corporation,
must be responsible for the treatment of the patient. This
is a principle that bar associations championed; indeed, the
impropriety of a lawyer's delegating his professional responsibility has long been a battle cry in the struggle of bar
associations against encroachment on the legal domain by
banks and trust companies, title companies and accounting
firms using lawyers as employees. Wouldn't the bar be compromised if it gave its imprimatur to association-corpora-
tions? But the temptations of tax savings through pension
plans and fringe benefits—and the dreams of some lawyers
that they might achieve capital gain on selling interests in
professional associations, or in retiring from an "association"—were too great to resist.

However, many lawyers felt that the laws regulating the
practice of the professions might prohibit the establishment
of a Kintner Association in a good many of the states. Consequently, they turned to the state legislatures to make professional associations more palatable and workable, and at
the same time provide a vehicle for coming in under the
corporate fringe-benefit umbrella. They succeeded with
astonishing speed; maybe that's because lawyers dominate
the legislatures. Special statutes permitting the formation
of professional associations have been adopted in nearly
two-thirds of the states.

The American Medical Association, that stalwart cham-
pion of individualized warm personal relationships between
doctor and patient, which adamantly opposes government-
financed medical plans for fear this delicate relationship may

be jeopardized, had no difficulty in approving medical practice by such associations. The high priests of the conscience of the American bar, the Committee on Professional Legal Ethics of the American Bar Association, was called upon to decide whether the newfangled association-corporation would collide with the Canons of Ethics. The Committee gave such associations its imprimatur by holding that although the Canons require that a lawyer's relation to his client be personal and that the lawyer's responsibility to his client be a direct one, there need be no conflict between the lawyer's maintaining his proper relation to his client and operating through an association-corporation.

These are not unrealistic positions of the AMA and ABA, since everybody, including the legislators who voted for the professional corporation bills, knew perfectly well that they are not really intended to alter anything except the Federal income tax. All the rest is really meaningless gibberish, insofar as the real world of doctor-patient, lawyer-client relations goes. Perhaps if professional corporations become widespread they may in time, as a new institutional device, have substantial effects on the relation of the professional to his client or patient, just as the Hollywood independent corporation now has a force that has suprised many of its creators. But for the moment at least, no real change in professional operations is intended through the use of the professional corporation. This is just a tax device to be winked at and used, hardly to be taken seriously otherwise.

Sham as an instrumentality, whether used by taxpayers in seeking to deceive the tax collector, or by state legislatures in laying the legal foundation for their constituents' desire to lower the taxes they pay Uncle Sam, must be approached as one would a woman of dubious virtue. Now, let me confess at the outset that I do not hold that sham is evil per se, or that it is never a legitimate instrument for dealing with legal, political or, indeed, personal problems. We have in the law an ancient and honorable device, resorted to by some of our greatest jurists, known as "fiction"; important developments in the law of equity took place through the device of fiction. We pretend things are what they are not in order to achieve justice; these fictions have been called the "white lies" of the law, for they are designed to promote justice. One of the most famous fictions in the law was the *"fictis legis Corneliae,"* promulgated by the Romans to enable citizens of Rome captured in the wars to dispose of their property by will. The fiction grew out of the established principle of Roman law that only a person who was a Roman citizen at his death could leave a valid will. It was likewise basic to the law that a Roman citizen who was captured by an enemy automatically lost his citizenship and hence could not have a valid will. To have modified either the principle that a noncitizen's will could be valid, or that captivity meant loss of citizenship was too much of a wrench for the Roman lawyers, and would have affected other legal relations. Instead, the *lex Cornelia* established the fiction that the Roman citizen's death occurred the moment he was captured; hence he died a Roman and his will stood. Yes, fiction has its place in the law, but it must be used with the utmost caution and only where the provocation warrants resort to subterfuge. The plight of professionals vis-a-vis pensions and fringe benefits hardly justifies resort to this device, although many lawyers apparently think it does.

The moral climate of the citizen in relation to his government is already in so deplorable a state that it is unfortunate that state legislatures enact laws which are designed to conceal the real economic facts behind a deliberately misleading legal front, in order to enable certain citizens to reduce taxes imposed by another branch of our government. If the professionals are entitled to fringe benefits, Congress should amend the law so as to extend these benefits to individual practitioners and partners. The state legislatures should not subvert state laws to help Federal tax avoidance. Indeed, there are those who believe that the Supreme Court will ultimately knock out the whole scheme and hold that the professional associations or corporations are still partnerships, and taxable as such.

A new chapter in the drive of professionals to obtain fringe benefits was written in the final hectic days of the 1962 session of Congress. An act was passed allowing individual proprietors and partners to set up pension plans which may include the proprietors of the business. They may defer tax on income used to buy annuities from an insurance company, to fund the plan with a bank or buy a new series of U.S. Government bonds. The funds may begin distribution to the parties when they are 59½ years of age, but distribution may not be postponed beyond 70½ years of age; and payment may be made to beneficiaries on the death of a covered person. Rather severe limits are placed on the deductible amounts. A proprietor or a partner with a 10 per cent or larger interest in the business may pay in up to 10 per cent of his earned income to the fund, but not over $2,500 a year; but he gets a tax deduction for only half of what is put into the plan for him. As is true with corporate plans, employees must also be covered; the rule under the law for individuals and partners is that all employees who have worked for the individual or the firm for over three years must be covered.

This bill was a severe disappointment to many of the persons who have been working for years to obtain pension tax benefits for self-employed persons comparable to those allowed corporate executives. Their reaction is reflected in the observations of the authors of a monthly commentary on tax matters:

It is apparent from this skeleton outline that the mountain's decade of labor has indeed only brought forth a squeaky mouse. . . . Perhaps it is time for Congress to stop its practice of teasing taxpayers with token relief. If there is substantial inequity in the tax structure, there should be substantial relief; if the revenue system cannot afford relief the status quo is more desirable than petty tinkering which only overlays the Code with unnecessary complexity.

Whether the new law will take the steam out of the drive to organize professionals into pseudo-corporations remains to be seen. Far more generous pension plans, with substantially greater tax benefits to proprietors and considerably more flexibility, can be set up by the professional corporations; and besides, they can also provide Blue Cross and Blue Shield, group life insurance and the whole gamut of other fringe benefits of corporations. Undoubtedly, there will be pressure on Congress at future sessions to liberalize the new law for the self-employed.

In the meantime, we have a new arrival on the legal horizon, the professional corporation, and undoubtedly some professional partnerships over the country will utilize this new device, at least until Congress gives them more favorable fringe benefit treatment. Whatever the eventual results of this ingenious device for giving professionals the benefits of the corporate vehicle for fringe benefit and other tax purposes—and we may not know the result for years to come, while litigation wends its way through the courts—it illustrates how far legal entities can be turned and twisted to unorthodox uses for tax purposes.

These then are some of the more dramatic uses and abuses of the corporation to obtain tax advantage. I believe that a fundamental change in the income-tax law is required, more far reaching than the patchwork loophole-closing attempts made by Congress up to now, if we are to deal effectively with the subversion of the corporation as a device for avoiding taxes. Because the required changes involve a reconsideration of the over-all methods by which we tax smaller business enterprises, I propose now to turn to that topic.

CHAPTER 6

Taxation of Smaller Business

The key weakness in our business-tax structure is that we have applied a Procrustean approach to businesses. By and large, we have sought to fit all corporations into a single tax pattern and all unincorporated businesses (except for those with legal characteristics of corporations) into another pattern. Therein lies the mischief that has resulted. An equitable and workable business tax requires that lines be drawn by economic factors, not by the form of legal organization. The whole gamut of devices for tax avoidance through the use of the corporation, described in the preceding chapter, stems from the tax lines drawn by reference to the form of legal organization. If we reorient our tax business structure by drawing economic lines, much of the artificial advantage and discrimination, the caprice and arbitrariness that obtain in business income taxation could be cured.

To cut out the opportunities for most of these tax devices, and to move from legalistic to economic bases for drawing tax lines, I suggest that the present corporate scheme of taxation (amplified by an undistributed-profits tax) be confined to larger businesses, incorporated or unincorporated, and that other businesses be taxed in the way in which partnerships and individual proprietorships are now taxed.

We have already observed that the tax law treats as corporations businesses which, though not incorporated, have the essential characteristics of a corporation. A good many substantial oil ventures have been able to operate without corporate tax. Real-estate syndicates of considerable size operate as partnerships. Large brokerage firms may operate as partnerships. These ventures, if they attain the magnitude of the larger enterprises we have described, ought to be subjected to corporation-stockholder taxes. They should pay a business enterprise tax at corporate rates, coupled with an undisturbed-profits tax, and a tax to the owners on distributed profits. Thus, we will come closer to achieving equality of taxation for economic equals.

The partnership mode of taxation commends itself for smaller enterprises, again whether incorporated or unincorporated. The reasons for continuing the double taxation of the business and the stockholders, as developed in our discussion of larger businesses, do not obtain in the case of smaller businesses. For the great bulk of smaller corporations, there is virtually no corporate tax under the present law because the earnings are largely taken out as salaries. But there is nevertheless a substantial number of smaller corporations that pay corporate taxes; in 1959, there were about 57,000 corporations that had net incomes of $50,000 to $1 million.

These corporations are not the giants that dominate our economic life; they are not typically able to administer prices so as to pass on corporate taxes to the consumer; they do not have ready access to the securities markets for investor's funds. Consequently, there is no economic reason for subjecting them to the double corporation-stockholder tax. Instead, the partnership mode of taxation is particularly adapted to such smaller businesses. Under the partnership method of taxation, there is no tax on the business enterprise as such, and all the earnings of the business are taxed to the owners in accordance with their shares of ownership, regardless of whether the profits are actually distributed to them. The compliance and administrative reasons for rejecting the partnership method in dealing with larger corporations are far less serious impediments where we are dealing with smaller enterprises. The major stockholders of the smaller business, unlike those of the corporate giants, are typically the managing officers who control the corporation's decisions as to dividend policy. The capital structures are usually simpler than those of larger enterprises. The determination of the income of the venture is an easier task in a smaller business than in a large enterprise, and, as is true with partnerships, the tie-in of the audit of the tax returns of the individual owners with that of the business itself presents no formidable complications.

If we were to tax all businesses, other than the large enterprises with substantial aggregates of capital or large incomes, as individual proprietorships or partnerships, regardless of their form as corporations or associations, we would achieve a giant step on the road to equality of taxation for persons of like income. The man who renders services as a doctor, engineer, advertising man or corporate executive, and the business man who manufactures or sells goods, or operates a trucking or other business would be much more on a level of parity than under our present systems. All would be taxed as individuals on their shares of the income that their labor (and capital invested in their businesses) produces, whatever the form of organization.

As part of such a tax change, the unfair discriminations now existing in the fringe benefit area between executives of a corporation who own stock, and partners or individual entrepreneurs, ought to be eliminated. The tax benefits of pension plans, medical and health-insurance premiums, hospitalization, and other fringe benefits ought to be made equally available to owner-workers in the business, without regard to the form of legal organization. This would doubtless produce a withering away of the current rash of professional associations. Undoubtedly, in all these cases limitations as to amounts of deductions, extent of coverage and other safeguards are needed in order to prevent utilization of these provisions by owner-managers of smaller businesses, as a means of bailing out income on a nontaxed basis.

The partnership method of taxation would also undercut much of the existing manipulation utilizing the corporation as a vehicle for diverting personal-service income from taxation to the owners, and largely prevent the misuse of the corporation as a way of achieving capital-gains taxation. The reshaping of business taxation here suggested could also lend itself to the accomplishment of another important over-all economic objective—giving a tax preference to smaller businesses. We have long held the view that a healthy economy requires the encouragement of smaller businesses. The power of the large corporation to obtain capital from lending institutions and the public, its power through large orders to obtain lower prices for its supplies, its ability to produce goods cheaply through mass production, its capacity to create new products through extensive research and experimentation, and its ability to attract competent manpower, all put the small enterprise and the new venture at a great disadvantage in the market place. Through governmental loans at low interest rates, assistance in obtaining Government contracts, and other measures including taxation, we have sought to offset some of the economic disadvantages of small business seeking to compete with its larger and more powerful competitors. Our success has been limited, indeed, as the tide of mergers and concentration of power in the corporate giants continues.

Congress has always at least expressed a warm solicitude for small businesses, although some of its purported efforts to help small business have, wittingly or unwittingly, produced unadvertised, if not unanticipated, benefits to taxpayers hardly in that category. Thus, under 1962 rates, the 30 per cent tax on the first $25,000 of corporate income, while incomes above that figure were taxed at 52 per cent, is illustrative of the desire to aid small business. On the other hand, the much publicized aid to small businesses adopted in 1958 by giving closely held corporations an option to avoid the corporate tax and be taxed, for some purposes, like partnerships, has furnished a new tax-avoidance device for some businesses and their investors. This "small business relief" provision has proved a bonanza for corporations, large and small, that have experienced spectacular rises in real estate and certain other assets, so long as they are closely held companies. Indeed, some tax lawyers are chuckling over their belief that this change in the tax law offers a new escape from the collapsible corporation penalties. Moreover, its elective features permitting taxpayers to move in and out of the corporate method of taxation as tax advantages dictate, are an invitation to tax manipulation. We are here discussing a proposal of a very different order, a mandatory, not an elective provision, with lines drawn by reference to economic standards, such as the size of the business or its income, not the number of shareholders.

The proposal to tax smaller businesses as proprietorships or partnerships does, however, pose two serious problems in areas in which the smaller business, taxed as a proprietor-

ship, would be put at a disadvantage as compared with its
larger, more powerful counterpart, i.e., the tax on the retained earnings of the smaller business and the consequent
unavailability of the capital-gains outlet for realizing on such
earnings. These problems are in a sense two sides of the
same coin.

Suppose a physicist and an engineer develop a new type
of electrical conductor. They manage to obtain some capital
the first year or two; bugs in production result only in losses,
and more capital is scraped together. The third year they
begin to sell their product and earn money. But now they
need new or improved machinery. If they cannot pour their
earnings, after taking out what they need to live on, back
into the business, the venture may flounder. This is a fairly
typical tale of the small business that may eventually succeed.

Under the present tax law (at 1962 rates) by use of a
corporation, the parties can keep excess earnings in the business, with only a corporate tax of 30 per cent on the first
$25,000 of earnings and 52 per cent on the balance. Under
our partnership-taxation proposal, unless there are provisions designed to deal with this type of situation, the development of some smaller businesses might be stifled, because the high individual tax rates would make impossible
the accumulation of the requisite capital by the parties.

Moreover, the proposal to eliminate the corporate tax
on smaller corporations and to tax their stockholders as
partners also poses the difficulty that some investors would
be likely to shy away from smaller businesses, with the attendant risks of a new enterprise, if they had to pay tax
at ordinary rates on their shares of annual earnings. Some
capital-gain bait may be required to induce money to flow

into smaller businesses, rather than into the established, old-line companies.

These are serious and difficult problems, but they are of a character that the tax law frequently faces and deals with. We can carve out exceptions to the broad general rule. For example, to deal with the retained-earnings problem for the smaller business, we might limit the ordinary income tax to the owners of the business on the first $25,000 or $50,000 of income of the business to 30% (the 1962 rate on the first $25,000 of corporate income), or to 22%, the rate proposed on this bracket of corporate income by President Kennedy in his 1963 Tax Reduction and Reform Bill. And we could add a cumulative ceiling over a period of years of $100,000 to $250,000 of earnings taxed at this rate. The preferential first-bracket rate would apply only if the funds are ploughed back into and are used in the business, or in an expanded business. This would be a boon to the owners of the business, whether the physicist-engineer-managers or the investors. When a sellout of an interest in the business takes place, or it is liquidated, then the additional tax postponed during the development period could be collected from the owners, softened by an averaging provision.

If we taxed the profit on the sale of the stock or other proprietary interest in the business at ordinary income rates, with a provision for spreading the profit over the years the stock was held in order to avoid bunching of income, investors, particularly higher-bracket investors, might still find putting their money into new and smaller enterprises less attractive than investing in the larger corporate-taxed enterprises. As a greater sweetener to attract capital to smaller businesses, we could go further and hold out the attraction of a capital-gains tax to the investor, at our suggested top rate of 35 to 40 per cent on his untaxed profit on the sale.

In short, there are techniques if we choose to use them, for granting preferential tax treatment, and for making special allowances to meet the exigencies of economic needs tailored to the objectives we are seeking to achieve.

If such a plan were adopted, the investor would be in a more advantageous tax position by putting his money into a smaller nontaxed enterprise than in the established, larger taxable enterprise. The reason is, of course, that he would have all the advantages of postponing tax on at least a part of the undistributed income as it is earned, and of capital-gains treatment on a sale, *without the bite of the corporate or business enterprise tax*. Certainly, this ought to encourage a flow of funds into smaller enterprises.

But is it sound policy to grant investors in smaller businesses this highly favored treatment? This would intensify the already existing preferences in the tax law for income from property, as compared with service income. The physicist and engineer in our example, who developed the gadget the corporation is selling and in effect obtained their stock interest or other proprietary interest in the enterprise for little or no investment, would pay at full surtax rates on their salaries and on their shares of the income in the business reflected by their proprietary interest. Should they pay at full current income-tax rates when they sell their interests in the business, while the investor who put in capital may realize his profit at a capital-gains basis? Wouldn't this be a striking and inequitable discrimination against brains in favor of property? And if we yield to these arguments and allow the physicist or engineer to sell out with a capital gain, won't we destroy the very structure we're trying to build up? Wouldn't this be giving the law's imprimatur to converting service income into capital gain? If the physicist

and engineer, why not the entertainer and the boxer and the
doctor and the lawyer, with the attendant abuses of independent motion-picture companies, professional associations and so on? Do the economic considerations which
impel us to accept capital-gain treatment for the investor
apply to the physicist and the engineer?

This brings us to the much debated question—how far
does the income tax thwart productive effort? Many people
have indicted our steep rate schedule as deterring initiative
and enterprise, as discouraging entrepreneurs from devot-
ing their creative energies to developing new products, expanding businesses, and exploiting new markets. Why
should a man break his neck to establish a new business or
develop and market a new product when Uncle Sam gets
most of the income?

Economists in recent years have devoted a good deal of
attention to this elusive problem in human behavior: the
effects of taxes on work incentives. They have come up
with some rather surprising conclusions, surprising at least
to people who take it as self-evident that high tax rates sap
work incentives. The evidence suggests that high taxes are
both *incentives* and *disincentives* to work. Some people work
harder to earn more money when tax rates rise, while others
cut their productive efforts because of taxes. In a 1952 study
made in England and Wales, 1,400 industrial workers, selected at random, were asked how high taxes had affected
their work; about 25 per cent replied that they had cut
down their productive efforts because of the tax, but about
the same number declared that they were spurred on in
order to maintain their living standards. Substantially the
same results were found in a study of industrial workers
made by a British Royal Commission in 1954. The Commission concluded that "the levels of taxation within pres-

ent limits do not induce any significant proportion of the working population to modify their attitudes to their working behavior."

When we turn from industrial workers, who are generally in the lower tax brackets, to highly paid business executives and entrepreneurs, the evidence points to essentially the same conclusion. Professor Thomas Sanders of the Harvard Business School set out to try to find an answer to the effects of post World War II income-tax rates on the efforts of business men. He interviewed 160 business executives of both large and small corporations. Although he encountered a great deal of griping among these business men about high tax rates, he nevertheless found that, "The cases in which the evidence showed executives to be working harder were at least equal in number to those indicating less effort, and the former were more definitely recognizable as a tax influence."

Some 300 self-employed English solicitors and accountants were interviewed in 1956; nearly two-thirds of them paid income taxes running to top rates of over 50 per cent. Again, the researcher concluded that the disincentive force of steep taxes was about matched by their incentive to greater effort. It was only when the top rates reached 70 per cent or higher that three times as many persons reported that taxes had been a deterring force rather than an impelling force to drive ahead.

A more modest but, nevertheless, illuminating inquiry was made some years ago by Dr. Walter Heller, Chairman of the President's Council of Economic Advisers. He submitted a questionnaire to 78 members of a League of Women Voters group in Minnesota. Their husbands were generally business men or professionals. The women were asked, "As a result of the higher levels of income taxes now

in effect, does your husband work more, less, or the same as
he did when income taxes were lower?" None replied that
their husbands worked any "less," 50 replied that they
worked "the same," and 28 that they worked "more."

Finally, there was an interesting bit of testimony given
in 1955 to a Congressional Committee by the head of one
of America's largest industrial complexes, based on his own
experience and observation in big business. Mr. Crawford
H. Greenwalt, President of the Du Pont Company, argued
that high personal-income tax rates are a threat to American
industry and that the erosion through income taxes of financial incentives to work may jeopardize industry. Significantly, however, Mr. Greenwalt was careful to insist that
the facts he had actually observed indicated that taxes had
not yet produced any such adverse consequences; he was
worried only about future managements. He said:

I doubt that high personal taxation has had substantial effect
upon the performance of present-day management people. . . .
By the time a man has reached a position with eminence within
his organization, he is influenced importantly by his sense of
loyalty, his sense of obligation, a preoccupying interest in his
work, or, as has been unkindly suggested, by conditioned reflex.

Mr. Greenwalt's observations point up the complexity of
the interplay of factors affecting work motivations. We are
dealing not merely with an economic problem, but with
conduct that has profound biological, psychological and
sociological aspects as well. Certainly, the financial motive
is a major factor in men's work, and to the extent that tax
dollars cut into the financial return, work efforts will be
affected; but curiously, as the studies show, taxes may be as
much of a spur as a deterrent to greater effort.

Quite apart from income, however, we human animals
have a biological need to work. The deceptively alluring

advertisements of insurance companies showing John Smith reclining lazily on a boat in tropical waters, fishing rod in hand, while Mary beatifically stretches out sunning herself (all on a retirement annuity policy), may conceivably be a picture of a good life for some people who have had a lifetime of work. Actually, the students of geriatrics are increasingly discovering that such a life of idleness leaves much to be desired, even for our senior citizens. Certainly, it would be an empty bore for most people who are not of retirement age. Some years ago, a Gallup poll taken in Canada disclosed that nine out of ten people interviewed believed that life with work is more pleasant than life without work; only 14 per cent of the persons favoring work gave as their reason for working that "one has to work to live." The struggle, the tensions, the fulfillment of hopes and expectations, along with the inevitable frustrations and disappointments, are all part of the élan that underlies the drive to work. As Professor Sanders declared, "What all history goes to show is again confirmed by a good deal of evidence in this study, that difficulty, danger and strenuous effort are themselves incentives to many men."

The need to create is an impelling force in men's work. And each man has his own creative drive, from the biologist probing the inner secrets of the virus in a search for a cure for cancer, to a production man developing more efficient manufacturing methods, an advertising account executive opening the market for a new product, a Wall Street banker working out a merger of two businesses, to a man and his wife establishing their own little candy store. Indeed, one of the key lessons that our educators and mental therapists are trying to teach us is the great need to tap each man's creative powers, if we are to reduce personality maladjustments.

In our acquisitive society, prestige, status, influence in

the community are also powerful incentives back of the urge to build or expand a business. The prestige value of moving from the vice-presidency of a corporation to the presidency, or of expanding a small electronics firm to the point where its stock is sold over the counter, may be more important psychologically, in terms of recognition and the resulting standing and influence in the community, than the accompanying increased income, before or after taxes. And the desire for power is another key ego drive, whose satisfaction may outweigh financial considerations. To build up a business to the point where a top executive has 1,000 workers and associates instead of 100, with whom he deals in production, in labor relationships, where he has lawyers and accountants doing his bidding, and where his busy life is interrupted by the need to catch the afternoon plane to Washington to negotiate a Government contract—these are emoluments of a successful business that increase men's feeling of their self-worth and self-fulfillment, which cannot be measured in dollar terms.

All this suggests that there is little danger that we will thwart men's creative efforts in the laboratory or their productive energies in the factory or in the market place, if we fail to reward them (as we are proposing to do for the investor) with preferential capital-gain treatment, on a sale of interests in businesses resulting from their efforts. The engineer or businessman already lives pretty well on his current income, if it has reached the higher-income tax brackets whose deterrent effects we are considering. He has his home and his car and boat, and can send his children to college. It may be that all income-tax rates should be reduced and, indeed, we have suggested that the higher bracket rates ought to be cut for all taxpayers, at the same time as we eliminate many existing preferences and loopholes. If the rates were limited to a peak of 65 per cent, as proposed by President Kennedy, a man who sells out a business he has built up at a profit of $1 million, would still have over a third of a million dollars left after taxes. That may not be quite the American dream of the nineteenth century, when every entrepreneur aspired to be a millionaire, but such taxes would still leave a comfortable kitty to be invested in businesses that could produce capital gain.

Investors are in a very different position from the entrepreneur whose sweat or brain built up the business. The investor ordinarily obtains little satisfaction from a successful investment other than a money satisfaction—and all the not inconsiderable emoluments that accompany monetary success in our society, but they are still only money satisfactions. Consequently, if we are to attract investments to business, and particularly to the smaller business here under discussion, we appear to be forced to offer attractive after-tax financial returns to the investor, despite the resulting tax inequality. But in view of the powerful drives and rich nonmonetary rewards available to the venturer who risks his services in an enterprise, the additional monetary incentive of preferential capital-gain treatment does not appear to be an essential ingredient to his productive effort. Accordingly, there is no compulsion to compromise the principle of tax equality for the noninvestor entrepreneur in smaller business enterprises; there is no overriding economic reason to prefer him tax-wise over the doctor, the lawyer, the actor, or taxpayers generally.

If we are to accommodate our system of taxing business to the economic realities of the 1960s, we must gear the levy to the crucial differences between the several thousand large, powerful businesses that dominate our economic life, and all the rest. In carrying out this objective, it would seem advisable that our present mode of taxing corporations and their shareholders be retained only for the large ventures, strengthened, however, by the adoption of an undistributed-profits tax. But as to smaller businesses, we ought to employ the partnership mode of taxation. The pressing need of smaller businesses for retained earnings should be recognized by permitting earnings to be retained, within prescribed limits, without tax. Likewise, we would grant preferential capital-gains treatment to investors, in order to stimulate a flow of needed funds into smaller business. Such a refashioning of the taxation of business enterprises and their owners would, I believe, give us a more equitable income tax, one which would strengthen the economy and at the same time increase tax revenues.

CHAPTER 7

The Expense Account Society, Payola and Taxes

Taxes have their impact on our cultural patterns. There has grown up in our society an expense-account elite, membership in which is symbolized by the credit card, which enjoys privileges and comforts on tax-free dollars. An Internal Revenue Service study of 38,000 income-tax returns filed in 1960 revealed that tax deductions were claimed for $5.7 million in club dues, $2 million for theater tickets and similar amusements, over $1 million for hunting lodges and fishing camps, $2.6 million for yachts and $11.5 million for business gifts. Estimates of expense-account spending put the figure at $5 to $10 billion a year, with an annual reduction in Federal revenues of $1 to $2 billion.

Individual business and professional men, movie and TV stars, writers and a whole host of other fortunately situated taxpayers make deep cuts in their taxable incomes through the deduction of costs of entertainment, automobiles, apartments, travel and other expenditures which are intimately associated with personal living costs. And corporate executives and others have their club dues, restaurant bills, travel and a multitude of other expenses paid for them by the company, without reporting the payments as taxable income. The benefits that the company president derives from having a company car at his disposal for "business" purposes include driving to and from home and the office and "incidental" use over the weekend. He may also enjoy tax-free paid country club charges, and company retreats. So far as

Uncle Sam is concerned, this is phantom income and is not
reflected in the corporate officer's return, although the company obtains a tax deduction for the expenditures as business expenses.

Business men have had no trouble squaring these practices with their consciences. Yet, as a writer in the *New
York Times Magazine* put it:

> Seen from a distance, the group portrait of expense-account
> society presents a rather curious picture. To a great many people,
> it inevitably looks and will continue to look like the *society of
> kept men.*

"Payola" has also become a way of American life which
is related to expense-account living, since these emoluments
are typically not reported as income by the recipient, although they are deducted as business expenses by the payer.
From tickets for the customer or the buyer to the leading
musical comedy, the fights and the World Series, we have
moved on to TV sets and hi-fis, a fur coat "for the Mrs.,"
cars and cash kickbacks to the key man, whether he be the
purchasing agent or the disc jockey. A survey made by the
Ohio State University School of Journalism of 650 of
the country's largest industrial corporations, merchandisers,
banks and insurance companies brought replies that nearly
half regularly make gifts to customers, suppliers, prospects,
newspaper men and public officials. *Printers Ink* has estimated that this annual "giving" has burgeoned from $200
million a year among corporate businesses in 1950, to almost
$1 billion in 1960. All this has become a national habit, at
the expense of taxpayers generally.

Business payola, like expense-account living, has profound
significance to our way of life. The buyer who places his
firm's orders with the manufacturer's representative who

provides the largest kickback not only violates his duty to his employer, but also helps push up the price of goods to the consuming public.

The deductibility of business entertainment expenses and business gifts stems from an innocuous-appearing provision of the tax law, the provision that allows a deduction from gross income of the "ordinary and necessary" expenses of doing business. If we're taxable on our income, the expense of earning it ought to be deductible. Entertaining a customer, taking him to lunch or to the theater or a night club are traditional, established techniques for getting or keeping business, and have qualified under our law as deductible business expenses. Of course, the Government could draw fine lines and suggest that the salesman's own lunch, or the vice-president's own theater tickets or night-club chits are not expended on the buyer and perhaps should be disallowed. But a rather persuasive answer can be made that many corporate officers who dine with prospects at Charles' Restaurant, sit with them in $9.90 seats at Broadway musicals and wind up with fancy tabs at the Stork Club, would never go to such places at such prices except for the customer.

But this is only the beginning, for as so often happens in tax matters, the legitimate has been abused and has fostered the illegitimate. There was, for example, the case of a manufacturing company which maintained a luxurious $230,000 hunting and fishing lodge, on which it spent $50,000 to $70,000 a year. There, with streams stocked with trout and the nearby forest abundant with deer, the manufacturer entertained customers, also making the lodge available to its own key company personnel. These costs were

allowed as tax deductions. Another corporation used the
lure of a subtropical island, where it built its own luxurious
resort to get business and make life fuller for its executives.
Customers and key company personnel, along with their
families, lived like kings; they were transported to the island by airplane and cruised about on fishing trips, all at
company expense. For one year this company claimed as an
income-tax deduction over $450,000 as the annual expense
of these "business" facilities; the Tax Court cut the figure
down a bit, but still allowed $375,000.

As stated in a business publication by a former top executive of a large steel company:

Some companies are more widely known for their parties than
they are for their products. The occasions for business entertainment range all the way from two for lunch in the executive din-
ing room to several thousand in the ballroom of the big hotel,
with name bands, and orchids flown in from Hawaii for the
ladies.

Gone are the days when a salesman occasionally wined and
dined his favorite customer, or perhaps gave a small theater
party. Nowadays, when the deal gets big enough, the company
yacht weighs anchor and moves into position, the company
plane takes off for a duck blind in Arkansas, or the best hotel in
Miami throws open its doors to expectant dealers for a week
of continuous circus.

The distaff side is cut in, too, on both sides of the deal. How
the ladies love it! With jet travel what it is, those who were
getting a little tired of White Sulphur may now hope to look
in on Capri or the Riviera.

The unseen partner in all this largesse, of course, the man
who rides the afterdeck of the company yacht, co-pilots the
duck hunters' plane, sits by while the caviar is spooned out and
the *crepes suzettes* sizzle, the man who splits the check at the
night-spot and hands the big bill to the headwaiter, is none

other than Uncle Sam. Lights would go dim along the Strip in Las Vegas and chorus girls would be unemployed from New York to Los Angeles if it were not for that great modern invention, the tax deduction.

The simple provision of the tax law granting deductions for the ordinary and necessary expenses of business has proved inadequate to stem the massive tide of illegitimate deductions, despite the efforts of the Treasury to ferret out the unwarranted expenses. The courts have made the Treasury's efforts even more difficult by an all too generous conception of where the line should be drawn between personal and business expense. Thus, in one case the Government disallowed a $10,000 deduction taken by a corporation as the cost of redecorating the home of its top executive; it was no accident that he owned most of the corporation's stock. The corporation took the case to court and claimed that the house was used for business purposes; a jury allowed a $9,500 deduction.

The expense of a twelve-day paid vacation at Las Vegas by an officer-stockholder of a corporation and his wife, along with two guests they entertained, was allowed by a court as a business expense. The taxpayer claimed that he took the trip on business and that his wife had to go along. If his wife hadn't come, the customer's wife wouldn't have come, and the customer wouldn't go to Las Vegas without his wife. And so, by this self-serving chain reaction, the whole party became a deductible business affair.

And even the $16,000 cost of an African safari enjoyed by the president and principal stockholder of an Erie, Pennsylvania dairy, along with his wife, was allowed by the Tax Court as a legitimate business expense. The court accepted the notion that the safari made good advertising for the

business and, indeed, at low cost; it was purely coincidental
that the president loved to hunt big game.

Once we start with the premise, as our tax law has, that
any entertainment expense that's good for the business is
deductible, the doors are opened to extravagant living on untaxed dollars for a favored group of taxpayers. And by these
standards, the law is faced with a hopeless problem of sep-
arating the deductible from the nondeductible. Most people
don't keep detailed records of entertainment expenses and
most taxpayers, corporate or individual, who have business
expenses in the shady area between business and personal
costs, resolve most doubts in their own favor by overclaiming
their deductions; then they add as good measure a margin
for the Revenue Agent when he comes around to audit the
return. This is a widely understood and commonly accepted
practice. And the Treasury has been unable to cope with
over-generous estimates by taxpayers of business lunches,
home and night-club entertainment, the claimed use of cars
for business purposes, and so forth. Checks and credit-card
statements prove nothing other than that money was spent;
but the Treasury is at a loss to disprove the taxpayer's statement that he entertained valuable customers or prospects.
Moreover, the courts, recognizing that detailed records are
not usually kept, opened the flood gates wide in a 1930 case
involving the song writer, George M. Cohan, by holding
that the Treasury must accept a taxpayer's reasonable estimates of business expenses, where other proof is not available.

In his first tax-revision bill, in 1961, President John F.
Kennedy proposed that we take a new tack as to the allowance of travel and entertainment expenses and business gifts
as tax deductions. He asked Congress to disallow entirely as

deductions certain types of badly abused business-entertainment expenses, such as night-club, theater, country-club and prize-fight charges, the costs of hunting and fishing trips and the expenses of maintaining luxury "entertainment facilities," such as pleasure yachts and hunting lodges. The cost of business meals would be limited to $4 to $7 a day and expenses of business conventions and trips combined with pleasure junkets would be limited to the business portion of the trip. And in order further to curtail lush tax-deductible living while traveling on business, the President recommended that deductions for meals and lodging be limited to the $30 a day travel allowance permitted Federal employees. Under these proposals there would also be a tightening up of the allowance for the expenses of maintaining automobiles, airplanes, apartments and hotel suites used in part for business and in part for personal purposes. Finally, the President asked Congress to limit deductible business gifts to individuals to $10 per recipient. Secretary of the Treasury Dillon estimated that these proposals would add $250 million a year to Federal tax collections.

A look at the lines of attack used by taxpayers who might be hit by these proposed tax reforms is a fascinating study in political action. A storm of protest descended on the House Ways and Means Committee at its public hearings on President Kennedy's proposals. At the outset, the witnesses were quick to seek to disassociate themselves and their clients from those who abuse the proper limits of business expense—that was always "the other guy." Thus, we heard from the lips of a representative of the National Restaurant Association that "fraudulent, frivolous" claims of entertainment-expense deductions "offend us as greatly as any one." And from a spokesman for a hotel association,

"We do not in any way approve of the abuses that may have occurred in recent years when taxpayers have attempted to deduct as business expense the cost of an African safari, or the maintenance of yachts and hunting lodges."

Next came an ideological attack on the Treasury's restrictive entertainment-expense proposal. The measure, declared the restaurateurs' representative, embodies a "philosophy of regimentation"; no administration in Washington should arbitrarily decide for American businessmen what are reasonable entertainment expenses. Another critic declared that President Kennedy would "relegate businessmen to second-class citizenship," and that "businessmen are capable of living and working ethically and . . . are in no greater need of legislated morality than anyone else." Congress was told that the measure, if adopted, would result in the "confiscation of property" by the denial of proper business expenses and that a "fundamental issue of property rights of free men and free institutions . . . is at stake."

From assurances of virtuousness and appeal to basic principle, the witnesses then turned to a hardheaded economic ground for opposing restrictions on entertainment expenses and business gifts. The National Restaurant Association, estimating that over $2 billion a year is reported as business expenses for food and beverages principally as entertainment, pleaded that the loss of expense-account business would be "critical" for the restaurant business, that the $800 million in wages and tips of 200,000 employees in the business would be threatened. Dire predictions were made that this tightening up of entertainment-expense deductions would deal a "vital blow" to the $1 billion a year annual convention business of the country, that in urban centers, dependent on successful hotel operation, there would be a sharp rise in unemployment, failures in "small businesses" that supply hotels and business travelers, "staggering losses" in the operation of civic centers and auditoriums, and a "decline in the economy of the area." And a union in the entertainment field, the American Federation of Musicians, joined in the plea; it replied to the assertion that "lights would go dim along the Strip in Las Vegas and chorus girls would be unemployed from New York to Los Angeles, if it were not for that great modern invention, the tax deduction" by making the "simple observation that the same consequences would be visited upon the theaters, symphony and concert halls, restaurants and hotels throughout the country and upon the great artists, the culturally invaluable talents and the hundreds of thousands of decent American families those enterprises nourish."

Finally, came the argument of the technicians, the accountants and the tax lawyers. No new legislation is required, they argued; all the Treasury need do is to take effective measures to enforce the law. There was amazement expressed at the view of the Internal Revenue Service that it could not effectively enforce existing law. All that's needed is "better policing of expense accounts"; the "fair and effective enforcement of the law is always welcomed by honest taxpayers." As one witness for a trade association put the matter: "We think it unfair to keep the whole class after school because one bad boy shot a spitball at the teacher. Ferret out those guilty of abuse and mete out punishment according to existing law."

Citizens who favored the President's reform, as is typical with tax changes which will increase taxes, were, with a few refreshing exceptions, largely absent from the Congressional hearings. The AFL-CIO did, however, support the proposals, declaring that "we do not think that job oppor-

tunities in the entertainment field or in night clubs or
restaurants or the theaters ought to be dependent" on expense-account deductions which are "immoral and unethical." We also witnessed the unusual spectacle of a partner
in a leading national accounting firm attacking the deductible entertainment-expense fashion as an "ugly way of
life"; he added that "way down deep, if business in general
could get out from under the whole process and let merit
rather than entertainment prevail, business would welcome
doing so. An albatross would be removed from its neck."
And a dissident East Side Manhattan restaurateur, who
caters primarily to business people, scoffing at the "consist-
ent drone of platitudes, deceit" of his fellow businessmen,
attacked the "corporate mentality" which places the center
of competition in business "less around the economics of
quality and price, but more around the dinner table, the
cocktail party, the night club and the theater party," all "at
government expense." He attributed the low state of the
New York theater—"the majority of plays being produced
are musical-comedy extravaganzas completely devoid of any
content"—to the tastes of the expense-account audience and
he took his own industry to task for extravagant practices
and exorbitant prices, which most citizens can't pay but
which lure the expense-account business.

The suggestion that lavish business gifts and extravagant
entertainment have become an "albatross" around the neck
of business is borne out by the survey mentioned above
made by the Ohio State University School of Journalism. Presidents of 650 large industrial, insurance, commercial and banking firms were questioned about their firms'
Christmas giving. Under a promise of anonymity, about
one-fourth of the business executives replied, bluntly and
often with acrimony. Some called the practice "blackmail,"

"shakedown," which they could neither approve nor escape. They told of gifts ranging from trinkets to Cadillacs to $280,000 in cash, to the "loan of a yacht—liquored, fueled and girled"! Seven out of ten of the responding business executives didn't like the whole business.

The Treasury's proposal for disallowing business gifts as deductible expense was in essence adopted by Congress; the 1962 revenue act disallows deductions for gifts to any one individual of over $25 a year. But its proposals to restrict entertainment expenses were torn to shreds by Congress. What came out of Capitol Hill was in essence a reaffirmation of the rule that business-entertainment expenses are to be allowed, plus the adoption of some new standards for judging whether an expense is truly a business expense, and a tightening up of the records required to be kept to prove that the expenditures were actually made.

The new law restricts allowable entertainment expenses to those "directly related" to or "associated with, the active conduct of the taxpayer's trade or business." Where a taxpayer claims a deduction for an entertainment or an amusement or a recreational facility—presumably that includes yachts and vacation retreats and hunting lodges—to obtain any deduction at all, he must establish that the "facility" was used "primarily for the furtherance of the taxpayer's trade or business" and that it was "directly related to the active conduct" of the enterprise. The deductions claimed for the entertainment and the facilities provided may not in any event exceed the costs allocable to the business use. Incidentally, anyone who is disturbed by tax allowances for expenses for "immoral purposes" may take solace in the legislation, for the Senate Finance Committee report declares that no deduction whatever is to be allowed under the act for hiring call girls to entertain clients. In "no legitimate sense," avers the Committee, are "expenditures of this nature" . . . "directly related to or associated with the active conduct of a trade or business."

The new law will undoubtedly curtail some of the worst abuses in extravagant living off the income-tax gravy train. The costs of African safaris and fishing cruises will now be difficult, if not impossible, to sustain for most taxpayers. Moreover, the limitation of entertainment deductions to the portion of the costs spent on entertaining customers and business associates should prove useful in cutting down allowances. If a man takes three business guests and seven personal friends to Toots Shor's, he will get a deduction for only 30 per cent of the bill; and if he uses his yacht for pleasure 40 per cent of the time it is in operation and for business the other 60 per cent, he won't get a deduction for more than 60 per cent of the costs of the yacht.

A premium on shop talk is established by the 1962 law. The statute grants deductions for entertaining customers and business associates at restaurants, theaters, concerts, sport events and so on, so long as there is "substantial and bona fide business discussion" before, after or at the entertainment event. Henceforth, tax men will doubtless urge their clients to talk business at every turn, and will ask them to admonish their wives not to object to shop talk if they want to continue their accustomed style of living. Moreover, some men's wives will be horrified by the tax pressure to confine their entertainment to business guests.

Perhaps the most significant change in the entertainment-expense area will stem from the Congressional repeal of the so-called *"Cohan"* rule. For years Revenue Agents have been forced by this judge-created rule to accept freewheeling and largely unsupported estimates of entertainment and certain other business expenses. Under the *Cohan* rule, everybody played the game; business and professional men knew they were overestimating their expenses. Conventions grew up as to ranges of entertainment expense allowable for various levels of income and types of business. The object of the game was not to ascertain how much was actually spent legitimately, but rather how to achieve a measure of equality as to the amounts taxpayers should be allowed.

As a result of the legislative repeal of the *Cohan* rule, the Treasury announced that it will require record keeping and detailed information to support entertainment, travel and certain other expenses. This includes date, places, names of customers or business associates with whom business was discussed, the nature of the business, and receipts for expenditures in excess of $25. If these rules stick—a hue and cry against them has been raised by restaurants, hotels and others as to the impracticability and the wastefulness of such record keeping and a number of Congressmen are up in arms over the requirements—and if they are faithfully administered by Revenue Agents, there should be a drop in entertainment, travel and related expense deductions. Of course, it is true that the detailed record keeping required to substantiate entertainment and other expenses is a nuisance and time-consuming. So is the preparation of tax returns for that matter, but it is a necessary nuisance. In any event, I suspect that the real gripe of business men is not the cost and expense of record keeping—I have not heard business men oppose accelerated depreciation, despite the additional heavy accounting burdens imposed—but instead their realization that the new procedures are likely to produce disallowances of unsubstantiated amounts of nondeductible expenditures that they have been getting away with for years.

An amusing side light of the new substantiation rules exemplifies the old cliché that somebody always seem to profit from other people's woes. As soon as the Treasury announced the proposed new record-keeping rules, the Diners' Club rushed into print with a full-page advertisement in *The New York Times*; it had found a new reason for spending money the credit-card way. "Diners' Club receipts," it announced, "do constitute sufficient documentary evidence" to satisfy the Internal Revenue Service under the new rules.

To anyone seriously disturbed by our expense-account society, the new provisions furnish a highly unsatisfactory remedy for the ill. The standards are too vague and uncertain and will, I suspect, result in the continued allowance as tax-deductible of too much of what is in truth personal living expense. The Senate Finance Committee's statement that it intends to allow entertainment expenses incurred for the creation of "good will," makes it look as if the barn door may still be wide open.

The language of the new law dealing with allowances for meals and lodging while away from home is also suggestive of something less than a determined effort to cut down expense accounts to reasonable proportions. The House Ways and Means Committee had limited deductions for meals and lodging while away from home on business to "reasonable amounts," but the Senate found this restriction of the deduction to reasonable amounts unreasonable. The consequence is that the new law disallows only "lavish or extravagant" expenditures of this character; apparently they need not be reasonable in amount!

A law is, of course, no more effective than its administration. The rapid and successive retreats by the Commissioner of Internal Revenue from his originally announced entertainment expense regulations, under a barrage of criticism and propaganda by restaurateurs and other business interests and threats of repeal of the 1962 legislation by some Congressmen, raise serious questions as to whether any significant tightening of entertainment expense allowances will have been accomplished. Thus, the placating top tax collector has made it clear in the revised regulations that company yachts, hunting lodges and night clubs are within the range of acceptable business entertainment. Nice distinctions are drawn in the regulations between "socially motivated" and "commercially motivated" entertainment; and it becomes relevant whether the surroundings are "conducive" to business discussion. The IRS has determined that night clubs and large cocktail parties tend to have such "distracting influences" as to be debarred in the usual case, whereas cocktail lounges (without floor shows) and hotel bars furnish an appropriate business atmosphere. Home entertainment expenses will be allowed if the proper business motivation is present, but some people have wondered whether the distracting influence of young children will preclude the establishment of an atmosphere conducive to serving commercial needs. The widely expressed worry that the costs of the taxpayer's wife's entertainment at the theatre, or a night club, or elsewhere may not be deducted, along with the tab for the taxpayer, the customer and his wife, has been officially buried. Business men (and hotel men's lobbyists) have also been assured that conventions at Miami Beach, Sea Island and other resorts may carry on, at the Treasury's expense, pretty much as in the past. Indeed, it may be that the pre-1962 rules have been liberalized, for under the new IRS rules a taxpayer's transportation and living expenses on trips that combine business and pleasure, including trade conventions, are now explicitly made deductible if the jaunt lasts no longer than a week and the "play" time amounts to less than one-quarter of the time away. Moreover, the fears of business and professional men that the new law threatened one of their most cherished emoluments of the tax-deductible mode of life—the daily luncheon complete with cocktails and epicurean menus at the luxurious luncheon club—have likewise been allayed by the new rules. These expenses are deductible, we have been told by the IRS, so long as you lunch with your partner, or employee or business associate, and talk shop—not a very difficult condition to satisfy. And even the new rules as to record-keeping that were designed to ferret out abuses may not stick, for they are under attack from Congress. Indeed, during the summer of 1963, the House-Senate Joint Committee on Internal Revenue handed the Commissioner of Internal Revenue a 30-page list of objections to the record-keeping requirements. When the smoke clears, one wonders whether any substantial curtailment of the expense account abuse will have been effected by the 1962 law and whether the whole process of enacting new legislation, issuing new rules and then retreating under pressure from the taxpayers whose free-wheeling practices were to be curbed, accomplished anything significant other than to delude the public into believing that the abuses of expense account living had at long last been checked. One is left with the feeling expressed by Senators Paul Douglas of Illinois and Albert Gore of Tennessee, who, in dissenting from the approval of the legislation by the Senate Finance Committee, declared that "the committee has presented our sophisticated expense-account society with a blueprint for continued high living at Government expense."

There is one other aspect of the 1962 legislation and the new entertainment expense rules that is disquieting—they are likely to operate discriminatorily against the smaller business man. It's going to be a lot harder for the small, unsophisticated taxpayer to continue to deduct questionable entertainment expenses, but the large, sophisticated taxpayer will probably come out pretty well. The small entrepreneur doesn't have an accountant at his left to keep and build up his records of "business" expense, or a tax lawyer at his right to advise as to how each step can be taken most advantageously. Besides, his business contacts are necessarily limited, so that he may have difficulty in transforming his visits to the fights and night clubs and the weekends at his country place into business sessions, if he has to name his business guests and identify the deal discussed.

Now, contrast this with the officers of corporations of the size and variety of the functions and activities of the large automobile, oil, chemical and steel companies and the banks and insurance companies. An automobile company's yacht or an oil company's summer retreat could always have some persons on it who are involved in company business. Indeed, it might be difficult for executives of companies such as General Electric or Union Carbide to find people to entertain who do not do business or may not be prospects for dealing with the corporation. Such companies, with their well-staffed accounting departments, can afford to maintain meticulous records, and on advice of counsel at every step to seek to have them match impeccably the law's requirements. An innocuous-looking provision in the regulations dealing with the costs of transportation on combined business and pleasure trips and conventions, exemplifies the operation of the rules as applied to large and smaller businesses. If the trip lasts a week or longer, the taxpayer cannot deduct his transportation costs, but there is an exception from this rule if the taxpayer is an employee who had no "substantial control" over determining whether the trip should be taken; then the transportation costs are deductible, even if it's a six-week combined business and pleasure trip to Europe or an eight-week journey to the Far East. This means, I suppose, in a large corporation that if any officer, short of the President, takes the trip, the decision may be made by the President; and conceivably the President's trip may become tax deductible if matters are handled so that the Chairman of the Board exercises "control" over the decision. But if the Chairman of the Board, who enjoys big game hunting, would like to make a tour of a newly developed African country, it's not likely to be beyond the ingenuity of tax counsel to suggest that the Executive Committee meet and resolve that the Chairman ought to take the trip in the interests of the company. In short, in a widely held company, with a large number of executives and diversified interests throughout the country and the world, a plausible case for the deduction can be made out for almost any trip that any executive would like to take. But when you're dealing with the principal stockholder, who is also the principal executive officer of a smaller, closely held company, or a major partner in a business whose markets are narrow and products limited, the opportunities for extensive vacations in the guise of deductible business trips will be much more severely restricted. In short, all the odds are stacked in favor of the large, diversified, sophisticated, well-advised taxpayer and against the smaller, less sophisticated, ordinary business man. In a very real sense, therefore, the revised expense-account provisions will introduce new and unwarranted preferences and discriminations in the operation of the tax law.

The limitation of business gifts to $25 per donee is a measure of a different order; it is likely to cut deeply into payola. While there are some taxpayers who will doubtless succeed in burying TV sets or cars given to buyers' representatives in innocent-looking company accounts, this is an extreme of tax evasion that the great bulk of business management will be unwilling to resort to. Moreover, the disallowance of business gifts over $25 will give the business that wants to get this "albatross" of payola off its neck an excellent opportunity for doing so. This is the type of solution that we need to cure the expense-account abuse.

The President's proposals for curtailing deductions for entertainment expenses and business gifts would have meant a revenue gain of $250 million a year; as finally passed, the provisions will produce an estimated $60 million a year. Over-all the new law will undermine tax-financed payola and although it will have some beneficial effects in reducing inflated entertainment, travel and other allowances, it is not likely to make much of a dent in the expense-account mode of life, or on its corroding effects on our mores, our morals and the fisc.

CHAPTER 8

Tax Schizophrenia:
The Split-Income Tax Personality

Schizophrenia is a serious emotional disorder, but in the topsy-turvy world of income taxation, it is one of the marks of a happy adjustment to the taxation environment. We have traced the history of the development of the split-income system for married couples and have touched on the split-tax personality and its tax advantages in dealing with corporations, by splitting income between the individual and the corporation. Now we turn to a different facet of this technique, the further fractionizing of the income-tax personality within the family.

It all stems from the progressive tax-rate system. Take the case of Jones, a married man with taxable income of $35,000, after deductions and exemptions, whose wife has no income of her own. Jones and his wife would pay a tax of about $12,000 at 1962 rates; their top bracket would be 50 per cent, that is, the $3,000 of income from $32,000– $35,000 would be taxed at a 50 per cent rate. Jones' income is already split with his wife, so that he begins with two tax personalities; his income is actually taxed as if he and his wife had each earned $17,500. If Jones were single and had the same $35,000 of taxable income, he would have but one tax personality and would pay about $16,500 at 1962 rates; and his top bracket would be 65 per cent. The income-splitting of husband and wife takes income out of the top brackets and shifts it to a new bracket schedule of 20 per cent on the first $2,000, 22 per cent on the next $2,000, and so on. This is done by treating the income of husband and wife as belonging equally to the couple, no matter whose income it actually is. This is a complete reversal of the notion that long prevailed in British and American law that a married woman could not even own property.

All this was done explicitly by Congress and we may as well reconcile ourselves to the fact—even if we don't approve of the husband and wife split-income system—that it's here to stay. Married people in the income levels that benefit from the split-income system (millions of people with taxable incomes of husband and wife under about $3,500 to $4,000 a year get no benefit at all or virtually no benefit from the split-income system, because they would be in the lowest bracket without it) wield much of the political power in Congress. And they're not likely to be dislodged from their vested interest in the split-income system.

If being a dual personality saves taxes, why not become a triple or quadruple or quintuple tax personality and spread the income to lower and lower brackets? If a man has three children, he can cut his income tax, if he is willing to give income producing property to them. The children then own the property and the income belongs to them; each child has his own $600 exemption and standard deduction. Daddy needn't lose the exemption he claims for them as dependents, and most important of all, we start a new tax bracket for each child. Thus, if Jones holds securities or a piece of real estate, by transferring the property to the children, he can cut the over-all family tax bill.

There may, however, be a federal gift tax on the transfer of the property to the children. A husband and wife between them can make during their lifetimes gifts exempt from gift tax up to $60,000 of property; in addition, gifts to a child by husband or wife or both up to $6,000 a year don't count; they're excluded. After such gifts are made, a gift tax becomes payable, but in most cases of taxpayers in the brackets we're considering, that tax is worth paying. The gifts to the children will not only save annual income taxes (the gift tax is paid but once on the transfer), but they are likely to cut down estate taxes, on the donor's death, and they run higher than gift taxes.

However, giving property outright to children, particularly to minor children, presents complications and often brings on unfortunate consequences. There may be legal difficulties in selling the property if it is held by the children; there may have to be court accountings of the income and assets of the children; the parent may lose control over the free investment of the assets, even if he is the child's guardian. Usually the parent-donor will be the child's guardian, so that he can administer the property for the children; but the law imposes safeguards and restrictions on guardians that may unduly limit the father's freedom to invest the child's funds. And besides, when the child becomes twenty-one, the property is his, and if he chooses to buy a new Jaguar with the funds, Daddy cannot, as a matter of law at least, prevent it. So outright gifts, while attractive tax-wise have their shortcomings.

To have one's cake and eat it, too, the tax lawyers seized upon one of the most distinctive features of the Anglo-American law—the trust. The trust is an imaginative and flexible legal instrument, which was developed among the English propertied families as a way of disposing of wealth while retaining control of its use, and often of its later disposition. The trust has been characterized by the eminent English legal historian, Professor Maitland "as the greatest and most distinctive achievement performed by Englishmen in the field of jurisprudence." The origins of the trust device had nothing whatever to do with taxation, and long ante-date the Federal income-tax law. If a man dies leaving his widow real estate or securities or stock in the company he has built up, she may dissipate the funds for lack of finan-cial experience or sheer extravagance; she may be duped in her innocence, or the property may be transferred or willed to her second husband, instead of going to the decedent's heirs. Or if there is no widow, or she is well along in years, with the property going to the children under the husband's or the widow's will, few parents are prepared to consider, and fewer experienced lawyers will advise, allowing the chil-dren at age twenty-one to have complete control of sub-stantial wealth. If a child becomes the owner of $25,000 or $100,000 or $1 million worth of property at age twenty-one (which is the time the child must normally be given control of inherited property, if there is no trust), the child's de-velopment may be hurt by his having control of such wealth, wholly apart from the risks of dissipation of the funds, through extravagant living, or poor investment of the funds. Many lawyers can point to unfortunate cases of lives badly hurt and funds squandered or imprudently invested by widows or youngsters who were not protected from the ravages and responsibilities of their wealth.

The trust device gave the deceased greater control over his property, by vesting in the trustees he had selected the power to manage and control property and to direct the distribution and use of the property or its income. True, as is the case with all great reforms, the trust was abused and was used to tie up property and restrict its uses far beyond any reasonable requirements. Trustees are traditionally con-servative and unwilling to take risks and have prevented in-vestment in new ventures and stifled development. A dead

man could not predict the industrial revolution, the inter-
nationalization of trade or the electrical or electronic revolution; so that rigid trusts in the hands of conservative trustees
have sometimes seriously interfered with the proper use of
wealth. Both in England and in this country, legislation
developed over the centuries to curb the extent to which
property can be held in trust, and other provisions have been
made to curb the "dead hand" of trusts. Notwithstanding
these abuses of the reform, the trust is part of the warp and
woof of the English and American property system; it is
widely used and performs a highly important role in our
society. And a major contribution made by the United
States to the law of trusts was the development and acceptance of the corporation as a trustee. The trustees of estates
of magnitude are typically banks; indeed, that's where the
term "trust company" comes from, for banks are typically
banks and trust companies.

The trust was tailor-made as a device for splitting the tax
personality, while still controlling wealth and income. The
trustee is a separate legal person; he "owns" the property
and is generally taxable on the income it produces, unless he
distributes it to the beneficiary; if he does, the beneficiary is
ordinarily taxable. This legal situation fits exquisitely into
the tax-avoidance picture, for now, to go back to our earlier
illustration, we can have not only Jones and his wife—two
tax personalities—but also the trustee and the beneficiary or
beneficiaries as new splinter personalities. If Jones has three
children, he can split his income eight ways; income from
the property can go to six taxpayers, three children and
three trustees, and his salary and other income to himself
and his wife. And we can multiply tax personalities by
creating more than one trust for the same beneficiaries.
About all that's needed is reams of legal-size paper and

minor variations in the trust instrument. There can be one trust for each child, another for each child and the spouse, another for child No. 1 and child No. 2, and so forth.

This multiplication of trusts for men of wealth is by no means fanciful, for in the 1937 Congressional tax-avoidance investigation, it was reported that one thrifty taxpayer had formed sixty-four trusts for the benefit of four members of his family, at a tax saving of $485,000 in one year. Another couple set up forty trusts for their relatives, and a prominent lawyer and his wife used sixteen trusts.

A memorandum issued by a loose-leaf tax service, declaring that it was "prepared for the successful businessman" whose "financial aspirations are above the ordinary," and who is "thinking in terms of accumulating a half-million dollars or more," offers a manual of tax-saving methods which it declares "are the foundation of virtually every fortune being built in America today." Family trusts are listed among the roads to fortune building. And family trusts are big chips in American life. In 1960 more than $62 billion in assets were held in personal trusts by banks as trustees.

Widespread tax avoidance through the use of trusts invited Congressional loophole-closing action. Over the years, Congress has set up a variety of safeguards to seek to prevent the taxpayer from using trusts so as to avoid tax on the income but still in effect remain the economic owner of the property, receive its income, or retain the power to control distribution of the income or the assets among beneficiaries, or reacquire the property. Likewise, Congress acted to curtail the use of trusts as a way of supporting a man's family without tax to him of the income of the trust. The theory is that if a man gets the income or the principal back in his own hands, or can decide which of his beneficiaries is to have the income or principal, or the income is used to meet his normal obligations to support his family, these powers or uses are equivalent to owning the property. That makes good sense, because the essence of property lies to a large extent in the use or the exercise of powers over the property and the use of the income it throws off. In such circumstances, the separate legal entity of the trust ought not be recognized and the creator of the trust ought to be taxed on the income.

Let us see how far Congress accomplished these objectives. The law declares that if a person creates a trust and the trustee can distribute the income to the creator, or the income is used to support his wife or minor children, then he is still taxable on its income. The trustee appointed by the creator of the trust is in this case disregarded for income-tax purposes. A trust to be recognized must be irrevocable; you can't play "potsi" by pretending to give away the property and then have the right to take it back; the property must generally speaking rest irrevocably in the trustee. Turning to the control of the income and property, a trust won't siphon off the creator's income for tax purposes if the creator can direct how the income or the corpus is to be distributed among his wife, children, or other beneficiaries. All this is presumably designed to require real divestment of the creator's interest and control of the property, and to strip him of his power of revocation, redistribution, or recapture of the income.

In actual application, the rules have become little more than a ritual to which the high priests of the tax law make formal obeisance, and then proceed to carry out what in essence Congress purported to prevent. Thus, while a man cannot determine who is to receive the income or corpus of the trust to be recognized, he can give his trustee the widest discretionary powers to make distribution. Indeed, in the trade we call these trusts "sprinkling trusts," for the donor's largess can be sprinkled like water from a hose among the beneficiaries, now on one side of the family, now on another. And who can be the trustees? The creator's bank or his lawyer or his broker qualify as "independent trustees" under the tax law. In actual practice, the independence of the trustee is usually the sheerest fiction; trustees are selected in the knowledge that they are expected to do the full bidding of the creator, and they seldom fail to do so, at least while the creator is alive. With the rarest of exceptions, the creator's wishes are carried out.

Experienced lawyers will attest that this is just as true of those formally "independent trustees," the trust companies, as of one's close friends. All you need do is protect the bank from liability and you are ordinarily assured of having your wishes carried out. Indeed, the "independence" of the trustee is usually compromised because of the business relations between the creator and the trust. The lawyer or banker or broker still wants the creator's business. The result is that the creator of the trust in the typical case, for all practical purposes, does exercise the trustee's powers in determining the distribution of the income. He is consulted on investments and his advice will, except in the case of highly speculative ventures, usually be followed.

The rule that a trust cannot be revocable by the creator, if it is to succeed in siphoning off taxation, is, likewise, to a considerable extent, a meaningless legalism. A trustee—again the creator's lawyer or a bank or a good friend—may be given unrestricted discretion to terminate the trust and distribute the assets as he sees fit to the named beneficiaries, including to the creator's wife. Suppose, after five years, the creator decides he'd like to have the assets of the trust. The trustee is so advised, the trust is terminated by the trustee and the assets go the creator's wife. To be sure, if the husband and wife have been divorced in the meantime, this won't do; or if the wife will be so legalistic as to want to treat the property as really hers, when nobody meant to do anything but cut down Uncle Sam's take, there can be trouble. And the unbelievably complicated so-called "five year throwback rule"—a jumbled jigsaw puzzle of chasing income and recalculating taxes of past years—may produce some income tax to the husband, if the last five years' income has not actually been distributed to the children. These are possible complications and they have given rise to a mountain of learning, which trust men and tax specialists must master; and while in some cases the parties cannot accomplish their desires, over-all there is a wide range of trust operation in which the creator can get the assets back to his wife.

Or turn to the matter of the use of the income for the creator's benefit. We are admonished by the tax law that the trust cannot be used to discharge the creator's obligation to support his wife and minor children, if he wants the tax benefits of a trust. Yet, here too there is plenty of elbow room. Suppose our hypothetical Jones is a married man with two children; he has income from his business or profession of $50,000 a year, and income from securities or real estate of $20,000 a year. By putting the securities or real estate into two trusts, with his wife and one child as beneficiaries of each trust, Jones can save over $6,000 a year in taxes and keep the entire income in the trusts until the child reaches age twenty-one. If the trusts are set up when the older child is eleven years old and kept in the trust until he reaches twenty-one, Jones can use the $30,000 fund he has built up in tax savings in the trust for the older child ($3,000 a year for ten years) plus the income, after taxes, that the money kept from Uncle Sam will earn, to pay for the child's education after he becomes twenty-one. If Jones's child enters college at the usual age of eighteen, the trust can be used to pay the child's college expenses for his last year, for his medical or legal training or his graduate work in the sciences or business, for the child's trip abroad, for his car at college graduation, for the wedding gift or the cost of setting up a professional office—all at Uncle Sam's expense. And once the child has reached twenty-one, the year-by-year income of the trust can, if desired, be distributed to him to meet the increasingly common contribution by parents to their children's support, after they are married and are starting their careers. This will make the tax savings even larger, because now the trustee and the youngster are separate legal persons, and we can often reduce the tax on the income of the trust by distributing only a part of the income and keeping the balance in the trust.

Finally, there is the *pièce de résistance* of the tax man's bag of gimmicks—the short-term trust. Here, we have a hole in the dike that makes the statutory safeguards against the use of trusts to avoid taxes little more than an exercise in meaningless double talk. Suppose, in the case put above, Jones would like to use the income from his securities to see his children through the last year of college and professional school, and meet the other expenses of cars and travel that he expects to have, but doesn't want to part permanently with the underlying assets. The short-term trust is the answer; a trust may be set up, for a period of ten years or more, under which the income will be taxed to the trustee or the beneficiaries (if it is distributed to them), and at the end of that time the underlying assets may come back to Jones. It works and, indeed, Congress adopted an explicit provision of the law sanctioning the device, with safeguards and restrictions that are not, however, major obstacles to accomplishing this piece of legerdemain. Consequently, the result is that the tax on the income can be siphoned off through a trust for a ten-year period or longer, without loss of the underlying property, and the income can be used for normal family expense purposes; and yet Jones is assured that he will get the underlying property back when the trust term ends. The short-term trust is truly the tax man's magic weapon.

The corporation and the trust are, we have seen, venerable instrumentalities of the law, which have been widely used as tax-saving devices. There is still another legal instrumentality in the law to which tax lawyers have turned to split the family tax personality and avoid taxes—the family partnership. The partnership is a peculiar animal in the law. Sometimes we treat it as a distinct legal personality, which as an entity carries on business, borrows money and hires employees. But for other purposes we treat it as a group of persons owning and operating a business in common, without a distinct legal personality of its own. This hybrid of the law has served the tax-conscious business man well. As income tax rates rose, and particularly during World War II, when incomes and tax rates skyrocketed, the family partnership emerged as an increasingly popular escape from high surtaxes.

We noted earlier that the law does not tax partnerships as such. Instead, it taxes each partner on his share of the income of the partnership at personal income-taxes rates. If a father makes his child his partner, he can split his income with the child and cut his tax bill. True, the income will belong to the child, but it can be accumulated and used, as in the Jones case, after he becomes twenty-one. There might be practical legal and business difficulties if a small child became a partner of a business; but once again the trust device comes into play, so that a trustee can be appointed to hold the child's partnership interest and act for him. Hence, we have Jones running his business, with the trustee for his minor children as his partner.

If Jones's business earns $50,000 a year and his three children each have a 10 per cent partnership interest, then Jones will be taxed only on $35,000 and each of the trusts on $5,000 of income. This will save the Jones family about $5,000 a year in taxes at 1962 rates. Repeated over a number of years, this tax saving can add up to a tidy sum for Jones and his family. And again, Jones's lawyer or his accountant or friend can be the trustee, who will be amenable to Jones' wishes in the investment of the funds and the use of the assets of the trust.

The Internal Revenue Service, concerned by the rapid development of family partnerships during World War II, attacked them as shams and tried to tax the creator-parent on the income paid to the trusts for the minor children. Some of these "partnerships" were bizarre indeed. There was the case, for example, of Charles Redd, who was the major partner (he owned 97 per cent of the firm and a cousin owned the other 3 per cent) in La Salle Livestock Company, cattle and sheep raisers in Utah and Colorado; the partnership also ran a general store. In addition, Redd had a half interest in another business from which he received substantial income. Redd took his wife and his four children, ranging in age from three months to seven years, into the business as "partners," by giving them parts of his interest in the business. The testimony of Redd's wife as to her participation in the business makes interesting reading:

Question: Now, do you participate in the management of the business of La Salle Livestock Company?
Answer: Well, I have been producing partners.
Question: Beg pardon.
Answer: I have been too busy producing partners so far.

Perhaps the most amusing case of all was that of the taxpayer who had to hold off setting up his family partnership because his prospective partner had not yet been born. But that didn't prevent his eager lawyer from preparing all the papers with the name and sex of the new partner left blank. One can visualize the anxious father, nervously pacing the hospital floor, awaiting the double blessing of the birth of both a child and a family partnership.

At first some courts refused to recognize the validity of such partnerships for tax purposes. They disregarded them as sham and unreal, unless the partner actually contributed services or capital that originated with him, not as a gift from his father. And the United States Supreme Court for a time followed this view. As a consequence, the Internal Revenue Service issued a large number of deficiency assessments to businesses that had prospered during the war years. As the cases poured into the Tax Court and the District Court, a good many judges found themselves troubled by the rules that had been developed. Perhaps the most telling argument for recognizing the family partnership for tax purposes, despite its unreality as an economic matter, was the treatment of the *family corporation* by the tax law. A man can operate his business through a corporation, give an infant some of his stock in trust and cut his tax on the dividends, and the Treasury doesn't attack the arrangement as a sham. Why discriminate against family partnerships? Some of the courts began to yield, and became more tolerant of family partnerships. Maybe it was the court's sympathy for people standing up in court who were now faced with big tax deficiencies, people who had been told by their tax advisers that this was a perfectly lawful and acceptable way of cutting taxes. Maybe it was the widespread feeling—after the initial flush of national readiness to sacrifice all to win the war—that wartime taxes were exceedingly high and very burdensome. Or maybe it was a second sober look at the basic legal issues involved in the discrimination between family partnerships and family corporations. Such factors have a decided influence on the course of judicial decision.

In 1949 the Supreme Court receded from its previous decision that had been the foundation for disregarding gift-created family partnerships with nonworking partners. In so doing, it withdrew into a cloud of obscure legal gobbledygook to the effect that if the parties really "intended" to create a partnership, it could not be ignored for tax purposes, regardless of the family-gift origin of the interest in the business or of the services of the partners. This left a hopeless mess to administer and the prospects of endless litigation.

Congress stepped into the picture to try to bring some order out of this chaos. It did make the rules clearer and more definite. It could have tightened the standards for recognition of a family partnership for income-tax purposes. Instead, it moved in the opposite direction; it gave its imprimatur to family income-splitting through the partnership device, so long as capital is a material factor in the production of the income. One other provision was adopted which is designed to safeguard the revenues. The donor-creator of the family partnership must be given a fair deal on the allowance for his services. Thus, if the father-donor is the chief executive of the business, he must receive as his income a reasonable salary for his services before the partnership income is distributed.

The net effect of all this judicial and legislative backing and filling is that the family partnership tax-avoidance device has been legitimatized (with some safeguards). And here, as we have seen elsewhere, the man of property is preferred over the man who works only with his hands or brain, without utilizing material capital in his business. The shoe manufacturer or the department store owner is permitted to cut his taxes by the use of the family partnership device, because capital is important in producing income in his operations. But the owner of an insurance agency, or a public relations firm, the engineer, and probably the advertising man cannot cut their taxes by taking their nonworking children into the business, for in their businesses, capital is not ordinarily a material income-producing factor. Doctors, lawyers, accountants and other professionals are typically barred from using the family partnership device for another reason—nonprofessionals usually are not permitted to be members of a professional partnership.

These distinctions in tax treatment, favoring the men of property, stem from an uncritical carryover to the tax law of property law conceptions, which ought to have little to do with tax policy. The results are capricious and arbitrary from the viewpoint of a fair distribution of the tax burden among taxpayers.

What can we do to reframe the income-tax law so as to close up these family tax loopholes and achieve a fairer distribution of the tax burden? I do not believe that we can deal effectively with family income-splitting devices, unless we tax the family as one taxpayer on the income derived from the family property and its business, where there have been intrafamily gifts (we could, if desired, retain the husband-wife split-income system). This would mean that the income of children living at home or still attending school or university, income derived from stocks, bonds, family corporations and partnerships, real estate, or other property arising from gifts by parents, would be treated as the income of the head of the family. It would not mean that Johnny's earnings from his summer work or that Mary's baby-sitting money would be taxed to Daddy. Nor would a child's income from U.S. baby bonds inherited from Grandpa be included in his parent's income. We are here concerned solely with the family income-splitting devices through gifts of income-producing assets by a parent to his children.

Like all tax measures, such a proposal would present its problems; thus, "family" would have to be defined. Broadly speaking, I have in mind parents with children living at home or still attending school or university. We would have to deal with families in which there has been a divorce or separation and consider whose property could be charged with taxes; we would have to cover "sales" to children that are in economic substance, gifts, plus a myriad of technical problems. But these are the usual grist in the mill of tax legislation and are in the province of the technicians. In broad sweep, I am suggesting that the root evil in family tax-splitting lies in intrafamily gifts of property, and that the way to get at this problem is to tax family income from such property to the parent. In short, the solution to family tax schizophrenia is to treat the family as a single, integrated tax personality in dealing with income from property transferred within the family.

CHAPTER 9

Taxation of American Business Abroad

The spreading of American business around the globe brought with it new tax problems for businessmen and the Government. We had to accommodate our tax system to the impact on American business of the taxes of other countries; else burdensome double international taxation of the same income might result.

American corporations have a large and expanding stake in factories, oil wells, mines and other business enterprises abroad. Investments in business operated abroad under American managerial control, as branches of an American corporation or through subsidiary corporations, often with local interests as partners, have grown from less than $12 billion in 1950 to nearly $35 billion at the end of 1961. The pace of foreign investment has been accelerating in recent years. In 1953–1955, capital outflow for new manufacturing plants, oil wells and other facilities amounted to about $½ billion a year; the figure about doubled for the next several years, and in 1960 and 1961, amounted to about $1½ billion each year.

These are "direct investments"—an American oil company develops petroleum wells and pipelines in Venezuela, or General Motors builds an automobile plant in France, or the Sheraton hotel chain organizes a subsidiary corporation to build and operate a new hotel in Jerusalem in collaboration with local Israeli interests. We differentiate these "direct investments" from normal portfolio stocks and bonds, whereby an American citizen or an American corporation purchases stock in a foreign steel or utility company as an investor, without taking on management or operating functions.

Direct investments of American corporations in foreign enterprises are handled essentially under two broad patterns—through branches or through subsidiary corporations. Singer Manufacturing Company is a leading example of the branch operations pattern. The company got its start in Connecticut in 1851, and developed into a renowned worldwide organization. The Singer man and his sewing machine have penetrated some of the most remote corners of the globe. The company established its first foreign factory in Scotland in 1867, spread to Germany in 1904 and to Russia in 1906. In its colorful history, Singer has weathered such traumatic blows as the confiscation of its entire business in the Russian empire following the Soviet revolution, a business that it valued at $100 million; and the dismantling of its factory in East Germany by the Russians following World War II. Today, it has manufacturing plants in Canada, South America, Western Europe, the Middle East and the Far East, and sells its products in still other areas.

Singer has maintained an extremely simple form of legal organization for its foreign operations. A single American subsidiary, Singer Sewing Machine Company, owns and operates the manufacturing and sales facilities as branches in the various countries. The net earnings of this American company doing business abroad are taxed by our income-tax law as they are earned; and it makes no difference whether the earnings are brought back to the United States or used in the foreign businesses for current needs or expansion; they are still taxed as they are earned.

The income of Singer Sewing Machine Company is also

taxed by the countries in which it is earned. Thus, in 1962, the West German profits were taxed at 51 per cent and the British profits at 53½ per cent; Italy levies its tax at 31 per cent, Belgium at 28½ per cent and Japan at 49 per cent. If the United States 1962 corporate income tax of 52 per cent were piled on top of the foreign taxes, there would be little or nothing left for the stockholders of the business. To avoid this double taxation, the United States has adopted the policy of reducing the American tax by the tax levied by the foreign country in which the business is carried on. Thus, on its British income, Singer will pay the United States no tax, for England will collect a 53½ per cent tax, but on its Italian income, it will pay Italy 31 per cent and the United States 21 per cent. Because there are variations in the determination of what is net income, and other differences in the tax laws of various countries, the foreign tax credit does not always produce a symmetry of a full tax, but in general that is the objective and the way it tends to work out.

The Singer company's form of legal organization and the tax consequences of its mode of operation are not, however, typical of the way American foreign business is conducted or taxed. Singer grew up before the American tax laws took a significant bite out of its income, and once having established itself through branches, there are many technical and administrative difficulties in the way of changing its mode of operation. The more typical form of organization for businesses operating abroad these days is more complicated and more sophisticated than Singer's operation and produces more advantageous tax results. The operations of Joy Manufacturing Company of Pittsburgh are illustrative of the more modern type of setup used to reduce American (and foreign) taxes. Joy manufactures mining and construction machinery and equipment and related products. Unlike Singer's directly owned branches, Joy operates through a number of subsidiary corporations, each organized under the laws of the particular foreign country in which a manufacturing plant is owned—Canada, Scotland, England, France, South Africa, Australia and Mexico. By using foreign subsidiaries, instead of operating as branches of the American corporation, Joy is able to postpone paying American taxes on its foreign earnings until those earnings are paid to the American parent company as dividends, interest on loans, or other taxable items.

The income tax rates (1962) of most of the countries in which Joy's manufacturing subsidiaries operate closely approximate those of the United States—France and Canada 50 per cent, England and Scotland 53½ per cent, and only Australia with a 40 per cent rate, South Africa with a 37½ per cent rate, and Mexico with a 31.2 per cent rate are significantly lower than the U.S. rate. Hence, mere deferment of American tax, while useful, would not make a deep cut in the eventual total tax bill. Yet, Joy Manufacturing Company's total American and foreign tax bill has approximated only about 33 per cent of the net income of the enterprise.

This was accomplished through a standard device employed by companies engaged in foreign operations, *a tax-haven company*. In 1957 Joy created a subsidiary, Joy International, which it incorporated in Panama. The International Company was established to "sell" all the exports of the parent company and the foreign manufacturing companies. Instead of selling their exports directly to their customers, as they formerly did, the American parent company, the British, French, South African and other foreign operating companies now go through the motions of routing their sales through the Panamanian subsidiary.

This Panamanian company serves two very useful tax purposes. First, profits are siphoned off from the manufacturing companies to International. When, for example, the British or French manufacturing subsidiaries sell to a sales subsidiary owned by the same parent company, there is a good deal of room for manipulating the price, so as to cut down on the profits earned by the subsidiaries; and these are countries with high tax rates. The sales subsidiary is the beneficiary of these earnings; its profits rise, but they are not taxable, since Panama has no income tax. Apparently, Joy has been quite successful in this type of tax finesse, for as Senator Gore recently observed in questioning the company's representative in hearings before the Senate Finance Committee, "the affairs of your company with respect to its overseas holdings have been managed so as to make the operations in high-tax countries show a bare profit, whereas the profit in tax-haven countries is maximized."

The other function of the "letter-drop company," as it is sometimes called, is to postpone—perhaps for many years— all American tax on the foreign earnings. Thus, Joy International, between 1958 and 1961 accumulated about $3.5 million in profits and it paid no dividends to its parent company. But the funds are by no means idle; they're right back where they came from (except to the extent that they came from handling export sales for the American parent), for Joy International has loaned the funds to the various manufacturing subsidiaries. Joy International, located in its Panamanian tax-free haven, can and does freely receive dividends from the various manufacturing subsidiaries, and applies them in the business where they are needed. If the dividends were paid up by the foreign manufacturing subsidiaries to the American parent company, Uncle Sam would collect American corporate tax. Our Panamanian neighbor makes it possible to block off this tax, and the funds are still available for use anywhere abroad.

One other method commonly employed to divert earnings from the tax gatherer in various countries to tax-haven companies has also been used to some extent by Joy International—the foreign manufacturing companies must pay the Panamanian company for "know-how," secret processes, the use of patents, providing personnel and a whole variety of technical and advisory services. Just how and when and for what consideration all these intangible and somewhat vague, but readily manipulable assets find their way from the parent company that developed them, and how and where the reasonableness of the prices paid for these services and property are determined, are matters that are customarily shrouded in a good deal of mystery.

The use of a tax-haven company has become standard practice for American businesses abroad. Indeed, just as Delaware—a state whose laws were designed to allow the maximum freewheeling and the minimum of liabilities of corporate promoters and officers at nominal corporate taxes—has been traditionally the corporate haven of American business, and as Nevada has become a divorce haven, so a number of foreign countries, Switzerland, Panama, Venezuela, the Bahamas, Liechtenstein and Liberia, have exercised their sovereign taxing powers in a way which facilitates avoidance of U.S. income tax by American businesses. In Switzerland alone there are over 1,000 foreign letter-drop or tax-haven companies of American enterprises (32 of which are motion-picture producing companies), and in Liberia at least 600 such companies. In the

obscure and unlikely town of Zug, Switzerland, 52 subsidiaries of American corporations were recently formed
within a period of a few months.

Many of the tax-haven companies are essentially paper
companies, performing no substantial function, and indeed, all the activities they perform would, except for tax
motivations, normally be handled by each manufacturing
company. In Joy's case, the International Company has no
office or employees in Panama, but it has set up its office
in Monte Carlo, famous for its gambling and high living,
though hardly a likely spot for an industrial company. The
42 employees located in the Monte Carlo office "handled"
over $20 million of export sales in 1961, scattered through-
out the North and South American continents, Western
Europe, Africa and Australia.

What's there in it for the tax-haven countries? Why do
they lend themselves to these operations, since, if they are
to serve their purpose, these countries must collect little or
no income tax? The answer is that they and their lawyers
and accountants and real-estate operators and others, profit
in a number of ways, just as their counterparts in Delaware
and Nevada have profited from their respective roles as a
corporate domicile and a divorce mill. There are offices that
must be rented, and at least small staffs and their families
who must be maintained, housed, dined, served and entertained. There are also filing fees and annual taxes that are
small for the large industrial enterprises involved, but still
not insignificant to a Panama or a Liechtenstein or a
Liberia.

Indeed, to give color to the reality of the foreign-based
company, to minimize the risk of its being disregarded as
a dummy for United States tax purposes, some companies
establish substantial staffs in the tax-haven country or in

some other spot. Actually, this is likely to mean transferring personnel from the United States or the foreign operating subsidiaries, who do just about what they always did, but now for a Swiss corporation employer instead of a French or German; it's all the same economic pocket anyhow. Only the formalities and the papers have changed, but all this does produce some activity, and business, employment and profits to the tax-haven countries. Apparently, no sovereign conscience blocks this international tax game, for there appear to be no standards of sovereign morality to inhibit countries from adapting their taxing systems—for a small consideration—so as to enable foreigners to circumvent the tax laws of other countries.

The foreign subsidiary is the vehicle through which the direct investments abroad of American companies are ordinarily handled, largely as a result of tax considerations. Indeed, it is mainly in the extractive industries, oil, iron, bauxite and others, that American corporations operate abroad through their own branches, without using foreign subsidiaries, and again the explanation lies in the tax factors. To reap the United States income-tax advantages of percentage depletion in offsetting profits from various sources, the oil wells or mines must be held by an American company. The oil and mining companies typically have not, therefore, interposed foreign subsidiaries between themselves and the depletable assets. And this has worked out advantageously for many American companies in the foreign oil and other extractive industries.

We do not have the full story as to how many foreign subsidiaries and tax-haven companies American corporations have set up; nor do we have accurate data as to how far those corporations have effectively deferred or reduced

American taxes. But we do have enough data to know that these corporations have grown by leaps and bounds and that, as a result, large and growing amounts of foreign income of American business are benefiting from reduced rates and tax deferrals. Thus, information collected in audits of a group of companies by the Internal Revenue Service turned up over 4,000 foreign subsidiaries of American companies incorporated between 1954 and 1959. Department of Commerce reports disclose that undistributed earnings for 1959 through 1961 of foreign subsidiaries of American companies amounted to from about $1 billion to $1¼ billion a year. We also know that foreign subsidiaries of American companies in Canada and Western Europe repatriate about 45 per cent of their earnings after foreign taxes, as compared with 53 per cent of dividends paid by domestic companies; and that the tax-haven companies repatriate only a small fraction of their earnings. If tax deferral were eliminated for subsidiaries of American companies abroad in all except the underdeveloped countries, the Treasury estimated (in 1962) that additional taxes of $140 million a year would be collected.

One other factor stands out in examining the burgeoning direct investments of American businesses in other countries—we have invested our private capital mostly in the highly developed countries, while our investments in the underdeveloped countries have been largely in extractive industries. Indeed, Canada alone accounts for about one-third of all our foreign direct investment; at the end of 1961, nearly $12 billion out of nearly $35 billion was invested in Canada; and Western Europe accounted for about $7.5 billion.

While we have invested about $8 billion in Latin America, it has not been to build new factories, as is true in

Canada and Western Europe; instead our Latin American funds have gone principally into mining and other industries, in which we are engaged in extracting natural resources from the earth, not in building manufacturing plants. Africa and Asia, and particularly the underdeveloped countries in those continents, account for a comparatively small part of foreign investments of American businesses, less than 10 per cent, and here, too, the extractive industries predominate.

It appears highly likely that this trend will continue in the immediate future in that American business will find its most attractive investments in the industrialized, more stable, developed countries, where there are skilled workers and a consumers' market, and in the extractive industries in Latin America. Indeed, the development of the European Common Market, with its tariff preferences and mobility of labor and other advantageous features, is already accelerating the pace at which American businesses are locating plants and other facilities within the common-market area.

It was in this setting of the dynamics and economics of foreign operations that President Kennedy proposed, in his 1961 tax program, that the deferral of taxes through the use of foreign subsidiaries be ended, except for companies operating in the underdeveloped countries—Latin America, the Middle East, Africa, Asia and other areas. The American parent company would be taxed on the income of its foreign subsidiaries (except for those in underdeveloped countries) when it is earned, regardless of when it is distributed; and our laws would be considerably tightened up so as to curtail the tax manipulations of tax-haven companies.

In pressing for this key change in the taxation of foreign income, President Kennedy and Secretary of the Treasury

Douglas Dillon went beyond tax policy and revenue considerations. They tied in the tax reform with the widely discussed problem of the balance of international payments and the heavy drain of gold in recent years from the United States Treasury.

A word of background about this problem in international relations may be useful. The drain of United States gold reserves in recent years has been a major preoccupation of fiscal experts in the Eisenhower and Kennedy administrations. We ended World War II as the world's major creditor nation. Through the Marshall Plan, military expenditures abroad, foreign aid, private investments abroad and tourism, the outflow of goods and capital to the rest of the world far exceeded the inflow into this country. The result has been a deficit in our world balance of payments; a country's balance of payments is the relationship between money flowing out of and into the country. During the years 1950 through 1960, our balance of payments deficit totalled over $25 billion and our gold supply was cut by $6.8 billion; by the end of 1960 United States gold assets had fallen to $17.5 billion. In 1960, the balance of payments deficit reached $4 billion; but it has been reduced since then by measures taken by the Federal Government to $2.6 billion for 1961 and $2.2 billion for 1962; the resulting gold loss was about $900 million a year. In the first quarter of 1963, however, the deficit rose once more to an annual rate of $3.2 billion.

Why has this large flow of gold and dollar balances to other countries occurred? Fundamental, of course, is the fact that the United States Government backs the dollar with gold in international trade. It stands ready to redeem for gold, dollar balances held by any foreign interest. Now, it is highly significant that the outflow of gold is not due to the fact that we are buying more goods and services abroad than we sell. Quite the contrary, during the years 1950–1959, we exported in goods and services $3½ billion more than we imported, so that we had a favorable balance of trade, which has continued in the 60s. We wound up with our deficit in international transactions for quite different reasons; the Federal Government made long-term loans and granted credits to other countries, as part of our foreign-aid program, totaling $5.5 billion during 1950–1959; and private business invested in foreign countries an additional $18 billion. These foreign-aid grants and loans, our military expenditures abroad, and the huge expansion of direct investment in plants and other assets abroad are at the root of the deficit in our balance of payments.

In reviewing the taxation of American business abroad, the Treasury took the position that the policy of deferring taxation of the income of foreign subsidiaries is contributing to our balance of payments deficit. The deferral, it argued, encourages the flow of capital abroad and, as we have seen, billions of dollars have gone into foreign operations of American business. The tax advantages of deferral deter the repatriation of the earnings of the foreign subsidiary.

As a consequence, more American capital has flowed into Canada and Western Europe every year since 1953 than has come back home in return through dividends, fees or export sales to these countries; and it is expected to take at least ten or fifteen years for the increased return on these investments to catch up with this drain. In the meantime, for the years ahead, these investments abroad constitute a drain on our dollar resources. By ending the deferral on profits of foreign subsidiaries in Canada and Western Europe and other developed countries, the Treasury hoped not only to equalize the taxation of domestic with foreign business, but also to reverse the net outflow of capital from business investments, since the tax incentive to keep funds abroad would be ended. A saving of about $500 million a year in the country's balance of payments was expected to flow from the ending of the tax deferral to foreign subsidiaries in developed countries.

The underdeveloped countries, however, present a somewhat different picture. If General Motors establishes a plant in France to sell cars in the European market, exports of cars made in the United States are likely to be reduced; and the reinvestment of the earnings of the French plant in a Belgian plant will produce no new flow of capital to the United States. But investments by American business in Latin America or other underdeveloped countries tend to have a different over-all effect. These are nonindustrialized areas; a new plant in Brazil is likely to result in a substantial continuing export of parts or materials to supply the new plant. A dollar of United States investment in Latin America or other undeveloped areas generates, according to the Treasury, about forty cents a year in exports, as contrasted with exports of three cents a year worth of raw materials and other items for every dollar invested in the developed areas. President Kennedy, accordingly, urged Congress to end tax deferral of income of foreign subsidiaries in the developed countries, but to retain it in the underdeveloped countries, and at the same time to tighten up the law so as to end the abuses of the tax-haven company.

Business men sprang to the defense of tax deferral and, indeed, renewed their drive to obtain a reduction in the corporate tax rate on income from foreign operations to 38 per cent. With their lawyers and accountants, they defended deferrals and tax-haven companies as essential to the conduct of foreign business by American enterprises. These tax concessions are necessary, they hold, if we are to encourage American businesses to build and equip plants abroad, where markets need to be developed and where governments are unstable and there is an ever-present danger of nationalization and confiscation of properties. If a 52 per cent tax cuts into earnings, even though they are not paid up as dividends, there will not be adequate funds for essential reinvestment and development of the enterprise. And as one businessman put it to a Congressional Committee, tax reduction for foreign business income is needed to enable "the Nation to meet the economic challenge now posed by the Soviet Union and . . . to demonstrate abroad the benefits of free enterprise."

A preferential tax rate is also pressed in order to enable American business to compete with European, Japanese and other businesses in the world markets. In the Netherlands, domestic corporations are in effect taxed only on income earned in the mother country. Belgium has cut its tax on foreign-source income to 8 per cent and 12 per cent. Profits earned abroad by Italian companies are exempt from the company and income tax; France, Switzerland and Denmark exempt or subject to reduced rates their taxes on foreign income. And British companies can use a domestic overseas corporation, which pays no tax until the funds are repatriated.

The advocates of a reduced rate of tax on foreign income deny the charge that they are seeking a tax preference and aver that what they are really seeking is neutrality in taxation. If American business is to compete successfully in the world marts, they say, we must be on a level of tax parity with the business men of other countries. We should, it is argued, accommodate our tax laws to achieve neutrality with the businesses of other countries with which we are in competition.

Finally, the critics of the proposal to tax undistributed income of foreign subsidiaries argue that the tax would be unconstitutional. The parent corporation, it is argued, has no income on which it can be taxed until a dividend is declared or the stock is sold. To tax the mere accretion in value of the stock through the increased earnings would, it is contended, be beyond the Congressional taxing power.

How should we view this controversial issue in Federal income taxation? There is ample basis for the notion that American businesses abroad ought to pay American taxes, whether they operate through branches or subsidiaries. These businesses receive widespread benefits and protection from the American government and are the beneficiaries of large expenditures of Federal funds. While modern diplomacy no longer sanctions the landing of the marines to protect the interests of American corporations abroad, we, nevertheless, do utilize the vast political and economic power of our Government to protect American business interests. Our foreign policy is deeply interlaced with concern for American business; our worldwide consular service is its handmaid. American businesses abroad have profited from our vast foreign military and economic aid. All these and other protections lay the foundation for our taxing the earnings of American companies doing business abroad. And we are by no means alone in this practice; Germany, Japan and Sweden tax their corporations on their foreign business incomes much as we do; Britain, while making deferment simpler through a British overseas corporation, taxes the income when it is repatriated; and many other countries tax foreign income, although at reduced rates.

The suggestion that it is in our national interest to adjust our tax system to the tax systems of other countries in order to assist American businesses located in those areas in selling goods is a startling one, indeed. Many countries have highly unprogressive tax systems, with a much heavier comparative burden on the masses of their people and a lighter burden on businesses and higher-income levels, than we do; these tax systems are offensive to the philosophy back of the tax structure of the American democracy.

Surely, the French, the West Germans, the Dutch and the Japanese ought not determine American tax policy. We do not fix our wage scales by the depressed wage scales of Japan, or by the rates paid workers in West Germany, despite pleas that we cannot compete in world trade with our present scales. It is no more in the national interest to grant broadside tax subsidies to General Motors or Union Carbide or General Electric and other companies with plants and operations abroad, so as to accommodate to the taxes payable by their foreign competitors, than it is to adjust our standard of living to the standards of the countries in which these companies do business.

Neutrality as between corporations at home and abroad ought to be the guiding principle of our tax laws, unless there are overriding considerations dictating a departure from this rule. Foreign operations do present a special problem, the risk of double taxation at home and by the foreign country where the income is earned. But we have largely solved that problem by yielding the tax to the country where it is earned, through the foreign tax credit, with the result that business is subject to but one tax on the income (except for special situations arising out of technical problems). The plea for tax deferral and for preferential rates is essentially a request for a subsidy. Deferral can be of enormous advantage; it is in effect an interest-free loan. If $1 million in taxes can be deferred for ten years—and indefinite deferral is possible with business expanding abroad —at 5 per cent a year of simple interest, that's a saving at the Treasury's expense of $500,000. With the hundreds of millions of dollars a year in unrepatriated earnings—and sums that are mounting yearly as American investment in the European Common Market and elsewhere grows—the deferral privilege can be a huge bonanza at the expense of other taxpayers.

Since 1942, we have had in force a preferential tax rate for American businesses operating in the Western hemisphere; there is a 14 per cent percentage point reduction that covers companies operating in Canada, Central America, South America and the West Indies. The evidence is highly inconclusive that this tax incentive has caused a flow of capital that would not otherwise have gone into underdeveloped Latin America. Is it likely that Venezuelan oil and Chilean copper would have been less exploited by American business without the tax reduction? Surely, a tax stimulation seems unnecessary in Canada, which can hardly be categorized as an undeveloped country; and it is to Canada that the greatest flow of American business capital has gone.

The trouble with over-all tax subsidies to foreign business, whether through deferral or a rate reduction, is that they're too crude an instrumentality to do a selective, discriminating job. Through such sweeping tax provisions, we subsidize the risky and the nonrisky business; the business that will increase American exports, and the business that will not; the business that will replace domestic products, and

the business which will have no such effect; the business
that will repatriate the bulk of its earnings over a period of
years, and the business that will repatriate little or no earnings for many years.

There is another aspect, too, of the subsidy of foreign
business income which should give us pause. The foreign
business operations of American industry are largely concentrated in the hands of the largest and most powerful
corporations in America. To subsidize foreign business operations is, therefore, to subsidize through tax cuts the small
group of large concentrations of American corporate wealth,
at the expense of the rest of American business and the body
of American taxpayers.

Nor do we need to be unduly disturbed by the suggestion
that a tax to the American corporate shareholder on the undistributed profits of its foreign operating subsidiary, or of
its base company in a tax-haven country, would be unconstitutional. We already tax American individual investors in
foreign personal holding companies on the income of the
corporations, whether or not it is actually paid out to them;
and that tax was sustained in the courts nearly twenty years
ago. It seems highly unlikely to me that the Supreme Court
would hold that Congress cannot treat an American corporation and the foreign subsidiaries through which it conducts business, as a single unitary business for tax purposes,
or otherwise tax its undistributed income to its controlling
stockholders.

There is a stronger argument for deferral in new and undeveloped countries, where risks are greater and where the
needs to build up funds may warrant subsidy. At least such
a measure would attempt to confine deferral to areas which
we are seeking to build up. But here, too, because of the
crudeness of the tax subsidy, such a provision ought to be

carefully circumscribed. If Standard Oil invests money to open a new oil field in Venezuela, or Kennecott Copper develops new mines in Peru, why should we give the company and its stockholders tax deferral? The exploitation of the natural resources of a foreign country seems a peculiarly inappropriate area for such a tax stimulus. Investment in a construction business to provide roads in Peru or housing in the Congo may be of a different order; our national interest in improving the standard of living in those countries, and the risks and difficulties involved, may require American help. But is the tax instrumentality our best method of accomplishing these results? Would Federal insurance of such an investment, or a loan to aid the project, or the use of Federal loans or grants in aid as a subsidy to the local projects be more appropriate? We have had a good deal of experience in recent years with Federal insurance of housing loans and Federal grants in aid as means of carrying out public projects. By such methods we could more effectively tailor the amount of the subsidy to the needs of the project, and discriminate between the worthy and unworthy objects of Federal largesse, the pressing and the less pressing, and avoid the crude and broad-sweep effects that typically characterize tax subsidy.

In short, we ought to go very slowly in using tax subsidy or preference to accomplish the objective of encouraging American business ventures abroad. In the final analysis, we must decide how far it is in the national interest to use Federal funds to encourage foreign businesses, and how we can most effectively accomplish that purpose and the development of the underdeveloped areas. Over-all, we have more refined methods and instrumentalities that are better adapted than tax deferrals or rate reductions to the accomplishment of these objectives, methods that can be applied to the particular needs of a specific area.

Moreover, it should not be forgotten that the great and pressing needs of the underdeveloped countries are not for Ford assembly plants for people who can't afford cars, or for Westinghouse refrigerators that are beyond their reach, but for sewers and roads and houses and schools and electric-power projects that private business cannot build and operate profitably in those countries. These are areas where American governmental funds are sorely needed, as loans or subsidies, to lay the foundation for a better standard of living of depressed peoples. We may be taking the wrong tack in emphasizing, at least for the 1960s, the build-up of Latin America and Asia and Africa through private business operations subsidized by government. Perhaps a decade or a generation from now, after we have helped these countries to develop the elementary public facilities and utilities they need—which American and other governmental aid probably must help provide—then it will be time enough to concern ourselves with assisting American private business to expand its factories and warehouses in the underdeveloped areas, through taxation or other means.

Congress held extensive hearings on President Kennedy's proposals to tax to American corporations the undistributed income of the foreign operating and tax-haven subsidiaries (except companies operating in underdeveloped countries). But it refused to budge on the basic deferral problem. It retained the existing deferment rule for undistributed earnings in developed, as well as underdeveloped, countries in the case of operating companies. It limited its reform in this area largely to tightening up the tax-haven loopholes through the use of sales, letter-drop and similar foreign-

based subsidiaries. It provided for taxing to American controlling stockholders—that includes parent corporations of
foreign subsidiaries—the income of foreign sales and service
companies, investment income, rents and royalties and other
types of income of foreign-based companies that have been
the vehicles for siphoning off income to tax-haven countries.
However, the new provisions generally do not apply to income of foreign companies from less developed countries, if
the profits are reinvested in such a country. Moreover, when
the stocks of such companies are sold, the profit growing out
of earnings that have not been taxed to the shareholder will
no longer qualify for capital-gains treatment.

The new law also tightened up the foreign tax credit provisions and dealt a blow at two popular devices used by
American individuals to escape ordinary income tax on investment income—foreign trusts and foreign investment
companies. These are badly needed repairs if the existing
deferral structure is to be retained. They will make flagrant
tax avoidance more difficult, in the case of the developed
countries. But Congress has left the real problem of deferral
of tax on foreign operating income untouched. For, as stated
by Senators Paul Douglas and Albert Gore, in their dissent
from the report of the Senate Finance Committee approving the measure, "Anything short of removal of the deferral
privilege, whereby U.S. taxation of profits earned abroad
may be indefinitely postponed," is but " 'piddling' with the
problem."

CHAPTER 10

American Citizens Working Abroad

"The 'Gary Cooper tax law' is doomed. . . . People like Gary Cooper, Humphrey Bogart, Gene Kelly and various others found they could go to Europe or Africa, do a picture or two, then bask in sunny tax immunity on the beach at Cannes. For some it was the beginning of a tidy fortune. But the flight from income taxes got too much notoriety. Congress acted." (*Business Week*, Aug. 1, 1953.)

This story of the migration of motion-picture stars to Europe and Africa from Hollywood's sprawling studios and its glamorous living is a telling illustration of how an innocent provision of the tax law, born of a noble desire to do justice among taxpayers, can be perverted by the febrile efforts of tax men to open new tax-avoidance routes for their affluent clients. How did it come about?

Fairly early in our income-tax history, in fact as far back as 1926, Congress exempted from tax, income earned abroad by citizens residing outside the United States. Thus, if an American engineer moved to Brazil, was employed in the local office of an American or Brazilian engineering firm and established his home and family there, it was felt that he ought not be taxed by the United States on his earnings from personal services rendered in Brazil. The exemption rule covered salaries, professional fees and other personal-service compensation actually earned outside the United States. The citizen residing abroad was still, however, taxable in the same way as any other citizen on income from property, such as dividends on stocks, nonpersonal service businesses, real estate and other assets.

Inevitably, these rules produced controversy—what is a "bona fide nonresident"? How do you distinguish a temporary stay abroad from a bona fide residence? An American contractor sent a team of employees to North Africa to supervise the building of a power plant; the job took twelve or thirteen months; these employees were taxable by the United States on the income earned in North Africa if they were American citizens because they were on temporary jobs. But if the team was sent to handle the North African power plant and other jobs for the company, and the parties indicated a desire to work abroad indefinitely, to set up homes abroad, and certainly if they took their families with them, their earnings were likely to be nontaxable. The courts were plagued with extensive litigation, and nice distinctions have developed in drawing the line between those who adopted more or less permanent residence abroad, and were exempt from United States tax, and those who were on temporary assignments and hence taxable.

In 1951, a new development in the law of taxation of American citizens residing abroad took place. After the end of World War II, with the Marshall Plan and far-flung foreign aid, the vast building and other operations of American businesses required to establish United States military bases abroad, and the expansion of American business in foreign countries, a rapid increase in American personnel working abroad took place. Many of the higher paid employees, on admittedly temporary jobs, chafed under the tax discrimination between them and other Americans who qualified as nonresidents. The "temporaries," it is true, enjoyed the benefits of the foreign tax credit; they were allowed to reduce their American taxes by any income taxes paid to the country in which they worked; but they were nevertheless caught with the higher of the two taxes, American or foreign. But the "permanents," working side by side with the newcomers, and often doing the same type of work, were subject only to the foreign tax; and often the foreign rates were much lower than the American rates.

Moreover, a comparison of the rates alone did not reveal the true tax differentials. The administration of the tax laws of many foreign countries is notoriously lax. In Latin America and in a good many European countries, it is fashionable to understate income or overstate deductions to an extent that, whatever we may think of tax compliance in this country, would shock even the most callous of our tax-paying public. Besides, corruption in dealing with government officials, including the tax collector, is so widespread, and so much a part of the daily operations of business and governments in some countries, that the actual tax bills paid by persons in high places or those regularly dealing with government officials is likely to bear only slight resemblance to the law on the books.

Apart from such practices of tax evasion—"tax evasion" refers to illegal or criminal violations of the tax laws, while "tax avoidance" refers to legal methods of cutting taxes— each country's tax laws, like our own, has its own crop of tax-avoidance opportunities. Thus, Americans residing in England have for years cut their British taxes through the use of an expense account and deposits at home. If an American citizen, who is an executive of an American chemical company's branch in England, is to receive $30,000 a year in salary and needs only $15,000 a year to live on, he can, for example, arrange with his employer to pay him $10,000 a year salary in England, plus a $5,000 a year expense account. The other $15,000 can be deposited to his account in a United States bank. He will be taxable in England only on the $10,000 salary received in England; the $5,000 in expense money and the $15,000 not received in England is not taxable at all under British rule. And as a bona fide nonresident of the United States, none of this income would have been taxable in this country. All this—from tax evasion that is illegal and immoral but widespread, to legal tax-avoidance methods open to nonresidents—produced a deep sense of discrimination among the new crop of Americans temporarily abroad after World War II.

Congress yielded to the pressure of American business men and administrators of foreign-aid programs, who complained that they were having trouble inducing men to go abroad to do needed temporary work. A new provision was passed that exempted from tax personal-service income earned abroad by citizens who spent as many as seventeen out of eighteen consecutive months on the job in another country, even though their jobs were temporary and they could not meet the tests of bona fide residence. This new exemption was admirably suited to the American executive who was sent abroad to open a new branch of an American business, to help set up a new factory, or to build a road, and who spent the requisite seventeen months abroad.

As so often happens in taxation, this apparently narrow change in the tax laws, designed to end discrimination, opened the door to totally unintended new tax-avoidance practices. Motion-picture and radio and TV stars found the eighteen-month deal the Santa Claus they had long been clamoring for; everybody who was anybody in Hollywood at once became enamored of pictures with foreign settings.

We began to hear American radio programs broadcast from the Caribbean. One prominent actor made a picture in Mexico during a six-week period within his eighteen-month sojourn that brought him $275,000 in U.S. tax-free income. Another actor earned $600,000 in motion pictures in France and other European countries under the new loophole. In many cases, the stay abroad was so rootless that the foreign governments collected no tax, with the result that some entertainment figures succeeded in avoiding both American and foreign taxes.

This flight from the United States and its taxes made juicy newspaper and magazine articles. Hollywood unions began to complain that their members were losing jobs because of the tax-inspired migration of motion-picture production. Congress intervened and in 1953 put a $20,000 ceiling on the exempt income of Americans working abroad under the eighteen-month provision.

In 1960, there were about 50,000 United States citizens living abroad, who claimed exemption for more than $500 million a year in income under the nonresident and the eighteen-month provisions. Most of these, over 40,000, claimed bona fide nonresidence and reported all their earnings as nontaxable income. Somewhat more than 300 taxpayers claimed exemption of foreign earnings of $50,000 or more. These included sales representatives in Germany and Thailand who had over $200,000 and $300,000 in exempt earnings; a corporate executive in Brazil claimed $839,000, one in Germany $172,000, one in Canada $137,000, and one in Japan $233,000; a lawyer in Hong Kong claimed $460,000 of nontaxable earnings; a C.P.A. in Venezuela excluded $116,000, and a cotton merchant in Brazil $154,000.

The motion-picture people are, of course, in a class by themselves. A screen writer residing in England reported $200,000 of exempt earnings for 1960, a motion-picture director in Italy excluded $161,000, and an actress who resided in an unnamed country claimed exemption for $996,000 for 1959. And then there was the actor residing in Switzerland with the true Midas touch; he and his wife reported nontaxable income between them of $2,200,000 for one year. This couple made and saved a fortune, for a United States tax on $2,000,000 of ordinary income of a married couple would have amounted to some $1,800,000. The Swiss taxes, if imposed at all, would be only a fraction of that amount.

In April, 1962, while the Senate Finance Committee was holding hearings on the tax bill in which the administration sought to change the rules of taxation of Americans residing or working abroad, a news story appeared in *The New York Times* which provoked considerable interest before the Committee. It read:

A small New York corporation with neither an office nor telephone is now trying, among other things, to work out tax advantages for best-selling authors.

If the corporation . . . succeeds, it could profoundly shake up the book industry, and might encourage more American writers to live abroad as "employees" of the corporation, thereby saving tremendous amounts on taxes.

"A $100,000-a-year writer working in the United States might net only $40,000 after deductions, exemptions and taxes," explained one of the founders of the corporation.

However, if he becomes an employee of the corporation and does his writing abroad, "his spendable income could jump to about $80,000."

This scheme springs from the unhappiness of authors that they cannot ordinarily take advantage of the eighteen-month bit, or the tax benefits of permanent residence abroad. The reason for this treatment of authors is that the foreign-income exemption provisions apply only to wages and salaries and other compensation for *personal services*. A motion-picture star doing a picture in Italy or Egypt for Warner Brothers, who is paid a salary or fee for his services, comes within the compensation for services contours of the exemption; and so does a screen writer who writes a play for Columbia Pictures on a salary or fee basis. In the recent popular novel "Youngblood Hawke," by Herman Wouk, a Hollywood agent tells Hawke, who is a novelist:

. . . you're absolutely insane if you don't do the foreign residence bit. I *know* I can get you a screenplay job. A salary you earn as a foreign resident is free of U.S. taxes. That's why Hollywood's turning into a ghost town. They're all over in Liechtenstein and France and Italy and Switzerland doing the foreign residence bit. . . . You may be the only American living in Europe who isn't doing the foreign residence bit.

Authors, however, who write novels are not treated under our law as rendering services for which they are paid. They are treated as creating literary property which they own, just as painters and sculptors create artistic property. The novelist ordinarily works for himself in writing a novel; he owns the literary property which he "licenses" for sale by his publisher; and he "licenses" or "sells" the motion-picture rights or theatrical or TV rights. The law treats him as a creator and dealer in property, not as an actor or director rendering services, or as a screen writer hired to work on the motion picture owned by the Hollywood company. The courts, as a result, have ruled that authors' royalties or "sales" receipts do not ordinarily fall within the nonresident's tax exemption or the eighteen-month physical-presence exemption.

By the use of a corporation which will pay the author for his services and presumably own his literary product, some ingenious, tax-conscious mind has sought to convert author's royalties into compensation for personal services, so as to obtain the benefit of the foreign personal-compensation exemption.

The whole matter of exempting Americans abroad from income tax came to the fore once more when President Kennedy asked Congress in 1961 to cut down on the exemption for income of American citizens earned abroad. The President wanted to cut out the exemption altogether in the case of developed countries, both for bona fide nonresidents and for persons working under the eighteen-month rule. This plan would put an end to the exemption for persons working in Europe, Canada and Japan. Only if a person worked in an underdeveloped country—such as the African, and most Asian and Latin American countries—would he benefit from the exemption rules. Under the President's proposal, the $20,000 ceiling would apply, in the case of underdeveloped countries, both to temporaries under the eighteen-month rule and to nonresidents. Apparently, the administration believes that ordinarily citizens should pay U.S. taxes on all their earnings regardless of their residence, but would grant limited exemption for earnings in underdeveloped countries because it is in our "national interest . . . that Americans skilled in industry, education, medicine, and other professions be encouraged to go to less developed countries and contribute to their economic growth."

Congress did not go as far as the administration desired. It did not draw any line between developed and underdeveloped countries, but it did adopt a proposal that will put a serious crimp in the use of foreign residence by motion picture and TV stars and writers as a means of reducing

U.S. income taxes; and it also cut down on the benefits to permanent nonresidents. The new law, which keeps the $20,000 limit under the eighteen-month working-abroad rule, limits the exempt income of the bona fide nonresident to $20,000 a year for the first three years of uninterrupted residence abroad, and to $35,000 a year thereafter. The exemptions continue to apply only to service income earned abroad.

If the principle is accepted that bona fide, permanent, nonresident citizens ought to be taxed on their incomes from foreign sources, but that foreign-service income ought to receive preferential treatment, then the Congressional solution makes a good deal of sense. By limiting the exempt amounts to $20,000 and $35,000, Congress has granted tax relief to most bona fide employees of American or foreign businesses working abroad. The law pretty effectively rules out by its dollar limitations the tax-free gravy train for motion-picture stars and free lancers who really still have their roots in this country and ought to pay full taxes here. True, the corporate executive in Brazil who paid no American tax on $839,000 and the salesman in Germany who excluded $200,000 from income in 1960 will be unhappy at this turn of events. But if exemption is an act of grace of Congress, which waived its legitimate claim to tax the income as a means of encouraging service abroad, a taxpayer in the higher brackets cannot properly complain too loudly about a dollar limitation on the exemption.

The new legislation will also make the use of a corporation-employer for authors residing abroad considerably less attractive than it might otherwise have been. Suppose that an American citizen is a screen-play writer, who usually receives $100,000 to write a screen play. He has been residing in Switzerland for over three years. Can he, under the new law, arrange with his motion-picture producer employer to pay him the $100,000 for a play at the rate of $35,000 a year for the first two years, and the remaining $30,000 for the third year, and thereby have the entire $100,000 exempt from tax? No, the law is so drawn that he would ordinarily be exempt only for the $35,000 received during the first year. Many so-called "deferred compensation" plans for nonresidents will have trouble under this provision. To revert to the case of the successful novelist dealing with a corporation-publisher, he will now be unable to write a novel in one year, and then if it's a smash hit, receive his "salary" over a period of years, and claim up to $35,000 a year of tax-exempt income. Broadly speaking, the best he will be able to do will be to get the benefit of $35,000 of exemption for one year.

Returning to the rationale back of the new legislation and of the administration's proposals, I should like to raise the basic question as to why a citizen permanently taking up residence abroad should be taxed on his income from sources outside this country. Why should there be a difference between a citizen who derives income from a nonpersonal-service business he builds up and operates in Italy or Japan, who is now fully taxable, and his American manager whose salary is nontaxable up to $35,000? While the rules of property law treat the novelist as the owner of a piece of literary property receiving royalties from his publisher, and the law regards the screen writer as an employee, what possible relevance does that have to the tax treatment to be accorded the novelist and the screen writer? Perhaps we ought to have some low-rate flat tax, for example, 10 per cent or 15 per cent (if the foreign tax credit otherwise allowable would not reduce the tax below such a figure) of income of any kind derived from foreign operations by a United States citizen who is a permanent resident abroad, as a *quid pro quo* for services that may be rendered by, or for benefits he may receive from, our government. But it seems a rather provincial view to tax citizens permanently residing abroad, and working or running businesses or maintaining property there, on the same basis as citizens who reside in the United States.

Temporary residence abroad is another matter. Here the taxation of foreign-service income seems not unreasonable, particularly so long as a credit for income taxes paid abroad is allowed. An American who goes on a temporary assignment to help build a dam still has his roots and connections in the United States. Full taxation seems entirely reasonable, with a credit for foreign taxes paid, unless some broader national policy dictates otherwise.

The Treasury's proposal to draw a line as to exemption of income earned abroad, between those working in underdeveloped and developed countries, is one that ought to be viewed with a good deal of skepticism. Would tax exemption have any significant impact in inducing the best talent —engineers and corporate executives, lawyers and sales representatives—to go to Saudi Arabia rather than England; and will an American corporation choose to send its talent to Asia rather than to Europe because of the employee's tax position? And certainly it is hard to see why a motion-picture star making a movie in the Congo should go untaxed, while his former Beverly Hills neighbor doing a picture in Italy pays tax. All this sounds like a pipe dream as a force designed to affect the growth of underdeveloped countries.

There is perhaps justification for limiting the exemption from United States income tax for citizens who are bona fide permanent nonresidents to a dollar ceiling, such as the $20,000 and $35,000 ceilings adopted by Congress, by an entirely different approach. The facts of life are such that it is extremely difficult for the Internal Revenue Service to establish that an actor or producer or corporate executive or lawyer, whose ties and relationships remain in this country and who intends to return here, is not, as he claims, a bona fide nonresident. The taxpayer can easily rig matters to his full advantage—the address he uses, the house he rents, the care with which he follows his lawyer's instructions to give up his church and club memberships in this country and join up abroad.

The motion-picture stars and free-lance writers are an excellent case in point. Since the Treasury is likely to come out on the short end of the stick on the issue of proof of nonresidence, and thus be unable to prevent the guise of nonresidence from being established by people whose roots are really in this country, perhaps a dollar limitation is the only effective device available to cure the abuse. Most, but not all, of the legitimate nonresidents will be protected, since their incomes will be under the $20,000 and $35,000 limits. This is practical expedience overriding principle, but it may be a wise solution. However, it is hard to find a justification for taxing the American citizen-resident of Paris who derives income from Parisian real estate, or from a business he owns in Marseilles, or from a stock investment in a Burgundian winery, while the American manager-employee of such a business obtains the exemption. Nor is there warrant for taxing the expatriated author on royalties he receives from a French edition of his novel marketed abroad, so long as the screen-play writer for a Hollywood studio can earn $35,000 of nontaxable income. Doubtless, the statutory definition of nonresident could be tightened up so as to draw the tax lines more tightly, but the legal differences in the origin of income, as between property and services, ought not produce differences in United States tax results, so long as the incomes of both groups of American citizens are rooted in foreign sources.

CHAPTER 11

The Tax Blessings of Charity

Business has its tax angles, and so does charity. Few educational institutions, hospitals or churches are likely to mount a drive for substantial funds these days without a tax man at their side to aid the fund raisers in exploiting the techniques for obtaining the tax benefits of charitable giving.

The encouragement of gifts to charitable, educational and religious organizations is a long-established policy of our tax laws. Such organizations—schools, hospitals, social-service agencies, art galleries, libraries and museums, and a host of other community organizations—are themselves exempt from income tax on their own income from investments and real estate. Indeed, they are also free of property tax (usually limited to property actually used in carrying on their exempt activities), and from sales taxes on goods they buy, and frequently from other taxes. The justification for exemption from taxation on their income (at least when they don't operate actual businesses) is that these organizations furnish the community services that the Federal, state or local government would otherwise be called upon to provide. If private schools and colleges, hospitals and social-service agencies, and other such institutions were taxed, they would have to cut down on the community services they render.

The exemption for religious organizations proceeds on a different premise, that they promote morality and thereby further the welfare of the state. It has been said that "the whole framework of our civilization would be severely threatened" without the influence of religion and that "religion and morality are essential to the very existence of the organic state." While the Bill of Rights in the First Amendment to the Federal Constitution enjoins Congress to "make no law respecting an establishment of religion," and the recent New York school-prayer case reflects the view that the Fourteenth Amendment imposes similar restrictions on the States, no Supreme Court decision has held that tax exemption granted to religious organizations runs afoul of constitutional requirements.

The Federal income-tax law carries out this traditional principle by granting exemption from the levy to organizations "organized and operated exclusively for religious, charitable, scientific, testing for public safety, literary or educational purposes, or for the prevention of cruelty to children or animals." This broad, sweeping exemption is limited by the requirements that the covered organizations may not engage substantially in the carrying on of propaganda or otherwise influencing legislation, nor may they participate in political campaigns on behalf of candidates for office.

Exempt organizations were held by the courts to be free to acquire and operate commercial businesses, either directly or through subsidiaries, so long as the profits of the enterprise were devoted to the exempt purposes. As a consequence, universities and other exempt organizations began to buy up companies in such varied areas as food, ceramics, leather goods, and automobile parts; and they operated them under their tax exemption blanket. As one wit put it, in commenting on the macaroni factory owned by a corporate agency of New York University Law School: "Harvard Law School may have the best faculty in the country, and Yale Law School may be superior in teaching jurisprudence, but there's not a law school in America that makes better macaroni than NYU."

Businessmen complained of this "unfair" tax-free competition and as a result, in 1950 Congress acted to tax exempt organizations and their subsidiaries on income derived from commercial ventures. However, Congress retained the exemption for income from investments in stocks, bonds, or real estate. Moreover, for reasons understandable only in the light of the politically sacrosanct position of churches in our society, churches were not subjected to these restrictive provisions. They alone among exempt organizations remain free to engage in competitive commercial businesses without income tax. The Christian Brothers of California, an order which operates a novitiate to train members of the Order and conducts Catholic parochial schools, sought to bring the income it derives from its winery and distillery within this exemption. The business is a substantial commercial operation; indeed, the Christian Brothers produce the largest selling domestic brandy in the United States. The court ruled that since the Order's principal activities, other than its commercial wine and brandy-making business, are educational, not religious, in character, the Order is not a church; consequently its commercial income was taxable.

The most significant development in our times affecting charitable and philanthropic organizations is the growth of the private foundation. Until comparatively recently, foundations set up to hold substantial wealth and distribute income or the underlying assets for educational, charitable and public welfare purposes, were an exclusive prerogative of the few immensely wealthy families, such as the Carnegies, the Rockefellers, the Mellons and the Fords. A major tax motivation to setting up the more recently established of these foundations was the estate tax, for a large part of the property of these families would have been absorbed by the tax. The great increase in the affluence of our society, and the sharp rise in income and estate tax rates, have made the private family foundation an important instrumentality, not merely for the very wealthy, but also for numerous just plain wealthy families.

The growth of the family foundation is reflected in a report by a Congressional Committee that, at the close of 1960, there were 45,000 foundations and charitable trusts in this country (the Foundation Library Center claims that this is an overstatement and that there are only 15,000); 524 foundations that were studied had total net assets of nearly $10 billion. While the Ford Foundation accounted for $2.2 billion, and the Rockefeller Foundation and the Rockefeller Bros. Fund for about $650 million, there are hundreds of smaller foundations, each of which holds a million dollars or more of assets.

Undoubtedly, private foundations have made notable contributions to community projects that governments would have been unlikely to undertake. These include the substantial financial aid to higher education and the far-flung experimental work in education of the Ford Fund for the Advancement of Education, and the pioneer work of many smaller foundations in such varied fields as scientific research, experimentation with behavioral problems, the development of mental-health clinics, the advancement of the theatre and the arts, and the protection of civil rights and liberties.

The private foundation serves as a vehicle for carrying out the donor's charitable and philanthropic objectives, but it also has other important uses. The donor can build up the income of the foundation from investments in stocks, bonds and real estate, without tax on the income; the organization can accumulate gifts from the donor up to his income-tax deductible ceiling, until such time as a desired substantial project can be financed. Moreover, the foundation is an effective instrumentality through which the creator can perpetuate the control of wealth within his family and his close associates far beyond his death, undiminished by deep-cutting estate or income taxes.

The operations of exempt charitable, educational, religious and other organizations, including private foundations, have not escaped criticism. In some quarters it has been suggested that the requirements for income-tax exemption ought to be accommodated to our current social attitudes, by denying exemption to universities, hospitals and other institutions that practice segregation or discrimination on the basis of race, color or national origin. It has been argued that a substantial scholarship program should be a prerequisite to income-tax exemption for private schools, prep schools and universities.

Moreover, it has been charged that some foundations have been used for private purposes. In some cases, income has been accumulated over a long period of years without devotion to the exempt purposes for which the organizations were formed; and through loans and investments by the foundations, the private businesses of the creators of the foundation have been expanded. Undoubtedly, we shall hear much more about the doings of exempt organizations, particularly the family foundations, in the years ahead. This is not the place to undertake an examination of the role and operations of exempt organizations, public and private. Our prime concern is with the other half of the coin, the income-tax aspects of gifts to exempt organizations, a subject to which we now turn.

The income-tax law grants deductions to both individuals and corporations for gifts to these exempt organizations. Again, the philosophy back of this allowance in the case of philanthropic and educational organizations is that the taxpayer, by making his contributions, is sharing the cost of what are essentially governmental and community services. Similar reasoning is back of the comparable provisions allowing exemptions from estate and inheritance taxes of property passed at death, not to one's heirs, but willed to an exempt organization.

For the year 1959, individuals gave $4.5 billion to exempt organizations and saved an estimated $1 billion in income taxes by so doing. During the ten-year period 1948 through 1957, annual individual charitable giving rose from $1.9 billion to $4.5 billion, which is a good deal more than incomes rose during this same period.

There is little doubt that the Federal income-tax deduction is a powerful incentive to charitable giving for taxpayers in upper brackets. The higher a man's bracket, the greater the incentive. Thus, if a man in the 60 per cent bracket gives $10,000 to his college, his actual out-of-pocket cost is only $4,000; and he has the personal gratification of having given a large sum to his alma mater, and perhaps of having his name placed on the honor plaque of donors in Old Main Hall.

The income-tax law generally puts a ceiling on deductible gifts, for Congress was unwilling to push charitable contributions to a point where a rich man could avoid most or all of his tax by large contributions. The ceiling on charitable gifts is 20 per cent of "adjusted gross income" (generally speaking adjusted gross income means salaries and investment income, net capital gains, and net income from businesses and professions). An additional 10 per cent of the adjusted gross may be given and taken as a deduction for amounts contributed to our society's most favored charities —churches, educational organizations and hospitals. Congress did eliminate the ceilings for wealthy individual taxpayers who habitually give to exempt organizations the bulk of their taxable incomes. If an individual's gifts to charity for the year and for eight out of the preceding ten years, plus the actual taxes paid for those years, come to over 90 per cent of his taxable income, then he may make unlimited deductible gifts to exempt organizations. The Treasury has asked Congress to repeal this unlimited-deduction provision, pointing out that some taxpayers with incomes amounting to several million dollars a year contribute nothing to the support of the Government under the income tax. Corporations are permitted to offset income by charitable contributions up to 5 per cent of their taxable incomes.

For most individual taxpayers, the 60 per cent who use the "standard deduction" of 10 per cent of the adjusted gross income or $1,000 (whichever is lower), the charitable contribution is tied into this over-all flat allowance. Taxes provide no encouragement to them to give, because they obtain the same flat deduction even if they give nothing to charity. But for the remaining 40 per cent of taxpayers who itemize their deductions, the tax advantage of the charitable deduction is very real in terms of tax dollars saved. And, of course, there are comparatively few taxpayers in the middle or higher brackets who use the standard deduction.

So much for the framework of the provisions of the income-tax law dealing with tax deductible contributions.

Now for the unavoidable gossamer and the inevitable abuses of the provisions.

Most college alumni have received literature in connection with their alma maters' fund drives, pointing to the tax advantages of gifts of property that has appreciated in value. An illustration based on a memorandum dealing with tax planning for gifts to Harvard College, issued in connection with its $86,000,000 fund-raising campaign begun in 1958, shows how it works:

A bachelor owns stock worth $10,000 which he bought for $2,000 several years ago. His taxable income puts him in the 60 per cent bracket. He would like to sell the stock and give the net proceeds to Harvard, or simply turn over the stock to the University. The method he uses can sharply affect both his tax and the amount Harvard will receive, as the following table shows:

	Sale of stock and gift to Harvard	Gift of stock
Market value of stock	$10,000	$10,000
Capital-gain tax (25 per cent of $8,000 profit)	2,000	—
Amount of gift	$ 8,000	$10,000
Reduction in donor's income tax by gift	4,800	6,000

By making a gift of the stock instead of selling it and turning over the cash, the donor avoids the capital-gain tax. Harvard will not pick up this tax if it decides to sell the stock, since it is not subject to income tax. And because there is no tax to pay on the gift of stock, the alumnus gives Harvard a larger gift (by $2,000) and hence obtains a larger charitable deduction.

The key to this device is that the capital-gains tax is avoided and that a charitable contribution is allowed for the appreciation in the value of the stock on which no tax has ever been paid; and none will be paid by anyone. The Treasury originally took the position in such cases that the charitable-contribution deduction ought to be limited to the cost of the property given, since the appreciation is not taxed, but in 1923 it reversed its position, so that for forty years the rule has been to allow as a deduction the full value of the gift, including the untaxed appreciation.

Some years ago a farmer's gift of 7,000 bushels of wheat to an organization called Food for Friendship raised an interesting charitable-contribution question. The farmer claimed the value of the wheat as a deduction. The Treasury took the position that since the wheat was the fruit of the farmer's operations, it was unlike a gift of stock or land, but an assignment of income on which the farmer should be taxed. It pointed out that the expenses of raising the wheat were allowed as deductions, and held that it would be unreasonable to allow the expenses of producing income without taxing the income on the gift of the wheat. The courts, however, upheld the wheat farmer and the Treasury has since acquiesced in the court's view that the farmer, although entitled to a contribution deduction for the value of the wheat, is not taxable on the making of the gift. However, the Internal Revenue Service now disallows the business expenses incurred or deducted in producing the contributed wheat or other product.

In connection with the deal made with Cuba's Fidel Castro for the exchange of prisoners, taken in the Bay of Pigs invasion, for drugs and food, a number of American businesses made large contributions of their products. The Internal Revenue Service ruled that charitable-contribution deductions would be allowed for the value of the goods donated; however, the businesses had to reduce their inventory by the cost of the goods sold, which roughly is likely to have the same effect as limiting the deduction to the value of the gift, less its cost to the producer-donor. Merck & Co., a large pharmaceutical house, contributed $2.5 million worth of drugs in the Cuban exchange. Because the value of the goods was substantially higher than their cost to the company, Merck & Co., according to a press report, saved more in taxes by making the gift than its own cost of the goods. This is possible only because the deduction is allowed for the value of the gift, not limited to the cost to the donor. The company announced that this saving will be donated to support medical education.

All sorts of ingenious variations flow from the two-pronged principle that a donor may obtain a charitable contribution deduction for the full value of the gift (the inventory-cost deduction rule does not apply to gifts of stocks and similar assets) and at the same time go untaxed on the appreciation in the value of the asset donated. Suppose a trustee of a hospital had bought stock for $3,000, which is now worth $10,000. He's willing to give the hospital the $7,000 unrealized profit he has in the stock, but he'd like to get back his $3,000 cost. He can sell the stock to the hospital at the bargain price of $3,000, his cost. The courts have held that in such a case, the trustee is making a gift of the $7,000 appreciation, and he can take his deduction for that amount. Since the price he's received for the stock is no more than his cost, he reports no taxable profit. Or if the stock is pledged for a $3,000 loan, the donor again has no income, because that's what he paid for the stock. He still obtains a charitable contribution deduction for the $7,000 appreciation in value that he has given away.

So long as the amount of the deduction is dependent on the value of the property given to charity, opportunities exist for increasing the tax savings by inflating the value of what's given. Hospital and community-center rummage shops are masters at this gentle art of helping their generous donors chisel on Uncle Sam. Here's one way it works: You have some old furniture or bric-a-brac or clothing you'd probably have to pay to have cleared out of your home. The rummage shop can use it; you telephone the shop, a driver picks up the articles and the rummage shop sends you a "valuation" that stretches values beyond any reasonable market value. You use that figure in taking your deduction, and usually the Revenue Agent is not likely to dispute the charity rummage shop's figures. The donor is happy and will remember the rummage shop in the future; only the U.S. Treasury suffers.

Recently, with the increased interest in art, something of a scandal in valuing art works given to charity has developed. High-bracket taxpayers have donated paintings to museums, universities and other institutions and have buttressed the generous tax deductions they have taken by letters from art dealers appraising the paintings. Unfortunately, works of art cannot be valued in the same way as corporate stocks, or even furniture, flexible though that may be. A painting bought for $200 a few years ago may actually have a possible buyer at $2,000, but how can the Revenue Agent really prove that the $7,500 valuation made by a reputable art dealer was a phony?

A recent case illuminates the problem. Hilla Rebay, an artist interested in nonobjective painting and the first Director of the Guggenheim Museum of nonobjective art in New York, contributed eight of her own paintings to several colleges during a five-year period. She claimed that these paintings had a total fair-market value of $169,000 and took charitable-contribution deductions by reference to the asserted values. The Internal Revenue Service held that four of the paintings had a fair-market value totalling $7,000 and that the other paintings had none whatever, and reduced the charitable contribution accordingly. Miss Rebay took the case to the Tax Court, which heard the testimony of art experts and agreed with the Government in its valuation of four of the paintings at $7,000, but allowed a total value of $2,300 for the other three paintings. Tax Court Judge Raum gallantly made clear in the opinion that the Court's conclusions in no sense reflected on the artistic or aesthetic merit of the paintings, as he upheld income-tax deficiencies running to over $100,000.

The Internal Revenue Service announced in 1962 that it would henceforth scrutinize closely the valuation of art works given to charity; the alarmed galleries and art dealers, fearing, as a Washington newsletter put it, "that continued abuses will lead to a law prohibiting such gifts," have set up an art dealers group to police and establish ethical standards for art appraisers.

What justification is there for granting a tax deduction for the full value of property given to charity without taxing the appreciation? It's widely accepted that gifts to charity ought to be encouraged, and that the tax deduction is a powerful incentive to such giving. But do we also need to allow escape from tax on the appreciation in value? The man who does not own stocks or paintings, and gives away cash that he earns, takes into income the full amount of cash he gives away before figuring his deduction. Why should the man who owns appreciated property that he can give away be in a more advantageous position tax-wise?

There is another discrimination in the operation of the
charitable gift provision; it discriminates against the person
who donates services, as compared with the person who
donates property, to charity. Suppose Danny Kaye or Bob
Hope were to perform on a television program for a charitable organization, as indeed they and many other entertainers do, without compensation, in order to help the
organization raise money. If the usual fee of such a television star were $2,000 for the performance, is he entitled
to a charitable contribution deduction for the value of his
services? The Internal Revenue Service holds that only gifts
of property are deductible, not gifts of services. A carpenter
who donated his time to build county civil-defense observation posts was denied a deduction under this rule, as would
be women who volunteer their services to hospitals and
churches.

The line between deductible gifts of property and nondeductible services posed this teasing question: when a
person donates blood to an exempt organization's blood
bank, is he giving away property? "No," said the Internal
Revenue Service, "he's just rendering a blood service," and
therefore obtains no deduction.

Why should the law distinguish between gifts of services
and gifts of property? Indeed, the line becomes very thin,
for if Martha Graham were to dance or Benny Goodman
play his clarinet without fee for a community-chest drive,
they would be denied tax deductions, whereas if Milton
Avery were to donate one of his paintings, or Richard Lip-
pold one of his pieces of sculpture, a deduction for the value
of the piece of art would be allowable.

It can be argued, of course, that the dancer and the clari-
netist have never taken into income their fees for their services, and, therefore, they ought not receive deductions for the

gifts. But the same holds true for the painter and sculptor; they have never taken into income the value of the paintings and sculpture which they may deduct as charitable contributions. Perhaps a more weighty reason for disallowing deductions for services donated is the magnitude of the administrative problems that would be presented, and the opportunities for tax avoidance that would be opened up if they were allowed. If every woman working as a volunteer in a church or hospital, or as a den mother for the Girl Scouts, and every man serving on a school board of trustees, or in a community-chest drive, were to be allowed a charitable deduction for the value of his services, the revenue losses would run into large figures. And pity the poor Revenue Agent trying to deflate the claimed value of Mrs. Jones's endless hours spent for the PTA, or Mr. Smith's intensive work on his college's building-fund drive, multiplied by millions of volunteer workers over the land! It seems reasonably clear that it is not feasible, even if it were wise, to cover contributed services in the charitable deduction. But we could still produce equality between gifts of services and property by limiting deductions for gifts to the donor's cost. Then, Merck & Co. would be getting a deduction only for its costs of producing the drugs contributed, and the artist would obtain no deduction for his painting (except for his costs of canvas, paint and frame).

There are other income-tax facets to gifts of services to charities. A series of radio broadcasts made in 1937 by Eleanor Roosevelt for the benefit of charity caused a flurry in Congress. Republican Congressman Hamilton Fish of New York, a bitter critic of President Franklin D. Roosevelt's policies, appeared before a Congressional Committee investigating tax evasion and avoidance and waved in the air a copy of Mrs. Roosevelt's contract for the broadcasts.

The contract called for ten broadcasts by Mrs. Roosevelt
on "Women of Today," and declared that "it is distinctly
understood . . . that . . . Mrs. Roosevelt shall not . . .
personally receive any compensation other than the $1.00
legal consideration." But the agreement also required the
commercial sponsor of the program to "mail to the American Friends Service Committee . . . a check in the sum
of $3,000 for each broadcast."

The Bureau of Internal Revenue had informally ruled
that Mrs. Roosevelt would receive no taxable income on
account of the broadcasts. Congressman Fish charged that
Mrs. Roosevelt had used a tax loophole to avoid the ceiling
limitations on charitable contributions. If she had received
the $30,000 directly and had donated that sum to the
Friends, she would have been subject to the ceiling, and presumably would have paid tax on at least part of the broadcast fees. Mr. Fish called the Committee's attention to the
President's message to Congress during the previous month,
in which Mr. Roosevelt had indicted loopholes in the income-tax law as immoral and unethical, and asked, if Mrs.
Roosevelt could avail herself of a "special loophole, why
couldn't Mr. John D. Rockefeller or any of the great contributors to charity do exactly the same thing." The answer
made to this question by the Internal Revenue Bureau was
that it had never claimed that a person who renders services
to a charity thereby receives taxable income, and that Mrs.
Roosevelt never had a right to any income. For years, the
receipts of professional baseball games that go to charity,
and fees of concert stars and lecturers that are paid to charities, had all been given similar treatment.

All this is true; yet slight variations in the formal arrangements from those made by Mrs. Roosevelt produce very
different tax results. Some years ago, the executive director

of a charitable organization agreed to appear on a TV prize show as a contestant. He made it clear to the producer of the show that if he won a prize, it must go to his employer-charity. When he won a prize, the Treasury ruled that he had received "constructive" income, and that he could obtain only a deduction for his gift, subject to the ceiling limits. Consequently, he presumably paid a tax as a result of the transaction. Or, if an entertainer makes a contract to appear on a television show for a $3,000 fee and the next day says to the sponsor, "Don't pay me anything, just send the check to my favorite charity," he, too, will probably have the fee taxed to him as income, and will be restricted to his charitable deduction. Economically, there's no real difference between these cases and Mrs. Roosevelt's doing broadcasts for fees that go to the American Friends Service Committee. The differences are purely formal; the tax results ought to be the same in these cases.

The tax aspects of charitable contributions are also affected by a principle of the tax law known as the "fruit and tree" doctrine. The metaphor that the owner of a tree cannot avoid tax on the fruit of the tree, unless he disposes of the tree itself, has played an important role in taxation. The application of the fruit and tree concept to charitable contributions may be illustrated by the case of interest coupons on a corporate bond. Suppose you own bonds issued by Consolidated Edison Company of New York. You cannot give the interest coupons to your son and avoid tax on the interest. So long as you own the tree (the corporate bonds), that yields the fruit (the interest), you cannot avoid tax on the income by giving away the fruit. Incidentally, the same principle applies to earnings; one cannot assign tax liability on the fruits of his labor by assigning the income.

Under this principle, an author who writes a novel or a dramatist a play, cannot escape tax on his royalties by giving them to charity. The tree that produced the fruit is a piece of literary property the author has created; so long as he owns the underlying literary property, the author will probably be taxed on the royalty income. The best that he can do is to offset the royalty income by a gift to charity of the dollars. But if the author gives the novel or the play itself to charity, before he has made a royalty deal with a publisher or a producer, an entirely different result obtains. That is because of the niceties of the law of property. A novel is a piece of literary property; if the author gives away the novel (not a royalty contract), he has disposed of the tree, not merely its fruit. Consequently, he obtains a deduction equal to the value of the property donated. If a fair estimate is that the novel will produce $25,000 in royalties, the author can now obtain a charitable contribution deduction of $25,000 (up to the ceiling limitations). And he has no income when the charity, acting through the author's agent, contracts with the author's publisher for the publication of the book under the terms the author would obtain. Authors can accomplish this result of no income, plus a deduction, because they create property. All this is akin to the gift of the farmer's wheat, or the drugs to Cuba or the appreciated stock to a college. Singers, dancers, entertainers, lawyers and architects can do no more than avoid the income on their services rendered to charity.

We have already referred, in discussing family rearrangements of property designed to cut taxes, to the wondrous ways of trusts. They are a bit like the Wonderful Land of Oz, where there is magic that obtains in few other areas of taxation. Trusts have also been used to achieve awe-inspiring results in the charitable deduction field.

The trust can be used to circumvent the fruit and the tree doctrine. In effect, by using a trust, income can be donated to charity without tax to the donor. If property is transferred to a trust under an arrangement whereby the income is payable to an exempt organization for at least ten years, the donor will avoid all tax on the income. True, he obtains no deduction for the income going to charity through the trust, but he has avoided the 20 per cent and 30 per cent limitations, for no part of the income of the trust is taxable to him, even though it amounts to more than the ceiling percentage. If he had not used a trust, the income from the assets in the trust would be taxable to him, and he would obtain a deduction for gifts to charity, but subject to his over-all donation limitations. At the end of ten years, the property may be returned to the creator and the trust ended.

With Congress' pet charities—churches, educational institutions and hospitals—an even shorter, two-year trust, may be used. A man may in effect assign to a charity through a trust the income of assets he holds, for as little as a two-year period, avoid tax on the income, cut through the ceiling percentages, and have the property revert to him at the end of the two-year or longer term. In commenting on this two-year trust provision, one tax adviser has written glowingly, "Notice how generous one can be when a sudden burst of income is anticipated."

These techniques for circumventing the ceilings on charitable gifts are useful and widely used. But there's even bigger game to be had in the forest. Suppose Mr. Contributor puts $100,000 worth of bonds into a trust for a museum, which will receive the income for ten years; the property will then go to the donor's grown children (it must not come back to the donor or his wife). Of course, Mr. Contributor pays no tax on the income of the trust, but now the law treats him as having made a gift of the value of ten-years' income. Consequently, he receives a deduction for the value of the income itself. If the bonds earn an average of 3½ per cent or $3,500 a year, he has given away $35,000; however, because the charity will get the income over a ten-year period, we "discount" the value of the gift. The present value of $35,000 spread evenly over ten years, is, according to Treasury tables, approximately $29,000. So, Mr. Contributor by this trust has gotten himself a deduction of $29,000 (subject to the ceilings), in addition to avoiding all tax on the income.

Some people labor under the impression that because of the tax laws, one can actually save money by losing money. A favorite misconception is the notion that "big corporations" deliberately lose money to save taxes. Ordinarily, this is nonsense, for if a corporation loses money, the maximum tax benefit it can receive (at a 52 per cent rate) is fifty-two cents on the dollar; it is still out of pocket forty-eight cents on the dollar. But in the charmed world of charitable contributions, it is possible in some circumstances to be money ahead by making a donation. A lecturer in taxation at a Midwestern law school has published a law-review article dealing with this device, entitled "How to Make Money by Giving It Away: Tax Consequences of Creating a Charitable Trust." He showed that if a donor is in about a 50 per cent bracket or higher, he will actually be ahead by using the type of ten-year charitable trust we have been describing. His tax bill will be cut by more than the income he would have had over the ten-year period, after taxes, had he not made the gift; and then the property comes back to his family. The author of the article, it should be noted, holds that this result is improper and that the law ought to be changed to disallow a charitable deduction for the value of the income interest given to charity. It's enough if the contributor divests himself of tax on the donated income.

In the trusts we have been considering, the donor gives to charity the income of the trust. But many people need or want the income on their stocks, bonds, or real estate. They, too, can use trusts for charity advantageously. Suppose a man owns property on which he'd like to receive the income, but he intends to give the property to charity at his death. If he makes the gift to charity in his will, it is true that he will have no estate tax on the property; but it would be nice if he could also obtain some tax benefit from the gift during his lifetime. Under the income-tax law, he can have both a lifetime tax benefit on a gift that takes effect at his death, and still retain the income while he lives.

The technique is this: create a trust which gives the donor the income from the assets so long as he lives, and provide that on his death, the assets will go to an exempt organization. The law holds that the creator of the trust is making a present gift of the "remainder" interest to charity, that is, the present value of the property the charity will ultimately receive. We discount the present value of the gift for the value of the income he will receive during his lifetime. Suppose you are fifty years of age and make a gift to a hospital of stock now worth $10,000 and paying dividends of $500 a year, and provide that you will receive the income as long as you live, and that then the property goes to the hospital. You would be held to be giving away $4,800 to the hospital; you'd have the income and still get a $4,800 charitable-gift deduction. The technique for accomplishing such a result is once more that flexible instrumentality of the law, the trust. By this stratagem, you've added a new dimension to your tax benefits, for you now have achieved a lifetime income-tax saving for a gift that economically takes effect at your death.

Parents with children approaching college age have learned a great deal about obscure colleges in areas remote from their homes, because of the intense competition for college admission. And tax men who have heard of few colleges outside the Ivy League and the Big Ten and the Rose Bowl competitors, are well acquainted with Pomona College, a small liberal arts college in Southern California. Pomona rose to fame in tax circles because it was the recipient of a ruling some years ago from the Commissioner of Internal Revenue that sanctioned a neat bit of tax casuistry.

Suppose you own $100,000 worth of securities that cost you $20,000. You are in a high-income tax bracket and would like to sell the securities and invest the proceeds in tax-exempt bonds, so that the interest will be tax free to you. You intend by your will to leave substantial property to your favorite college. If you sold the stock and invested in tax-exempts, you'd have a $20,000 capital-gain tax at the 25 per cent rate, and have left only $80,000 for investment in tax-exempts. If your college had made the sale, the tax on the profits would be avoided. Pomona College suggested to such donors that they transfer the securities to Pomona, as trustee; the college would then make the sale, invest in tax-exempts and pay the tax-exempt income to the donor for life. Ergo, the capital-gain tax disappears; the donor has exempt income on $100,000 of principal, not $80,000 after-tax income; and Pomona College will receive $100,000—not $80,000—when the donor dies! Everybody's happy, and even

Uncle Sam seemed satisfied, for his Internal Revenue Commissioner in 1958 sanctioned this plan.

The Pomona College device became so common and so widely publicized a method of avoiding tax on capital gain, and at the same time shifting from taxable to nontaxable income—not otherwise possible—that the Internal Revenue Commissioner recently announced that he will no longer follow the ruling, at least where there is evidence that a sale of the stocks was an integral part of the deal. The Commissioner now holds that the capital gain in such cases will be taxed to the donor, where the transaction occurred after the Pomona College ruling was overruled. A donor who uses this method and hopes to avoid capital gain will at least face a lawsuit.

There are a number of variations of the charitable devices we have been discussing. Instead of setting up a trust with appreciated property, the donor can obtain his income by buying an annuity from a charity. If the actuarial value of the annuity is no more than the donor's tax cost of the property, he realizes no income on the transaction and obtains a charitable contribution deduction for the appreciation. The Salvation Army has apparently used this method to attract donors, and has stressed the tax advantages of charitable annuities. Life insurance trusts also serve as a medium for improving the advantages of charitable giving.

Charity and philanthropy, the private hospital and university, the community-chest and welfare organization—all these are basic institutions in our way of life. True, they have been increasingly supported and supplemented by governmental funds, as we have broadened our notions of the welfare functions of the state. Nevertheless, few American communities could meet even the most pressing needs of their citizens without community health, welfare and educational institutions supported by private contributions. The tax benefits of charitable giving are undoubtedly a critical spur to the generosity of donors. But abuses have grown up in charitable giving, discriminations and preferences and unwarranted tax escapes exist which ought to be remedied. If we are to achieve a substantial measure of equality of tax treatment of the giver of cash and appreciated property, of the man who contributes services and the man who contributes property, then the law ought to be changed so as to eliminate the preferential treatment given to contributors of property. We could accomplish this result by limiting the deduction in the case of gifts of property to actual nondeducted cost. The owner of stock would obtain a deduction for no more than its cost to him. The wheat farmer and the drug manufacturer would have a deduction for the cost of raising the wheat or producing the drugs, less the costs they've already deducted as business expenses. The artist contributing an original painting would have a charitable deduction only for the cost of his canvas, paint and frame.

We could move in a quite different direction in an effort to achieve tax equality. We could allow the deduction for the full value of the charitable gift, as the law now does, but tax the donor for the untaxed appreciation in the property donated. The trouble with this solution is that it would produce inequality in reverse, for it would discriminate against the property given in favor of the contributor of services. The Metropolitan opera star who sings at a charity ball without fee would have no income and no deduction; but the artist contributing a painting, or the owner some shares of stock would realize taxable income from the gift, and could run into the ceiling limitations on the contribution. Consequently, if the law is to be changed, Congress ought to limit the charitable gift of property to the giver's undeducted costs.

I have tried out these observations on fund raisers, and every one I have talked to has thrown up his hands in horror at the notion that the law be changed to eliminate what I have regarded as abuses of charitable giving. They are particularly disturbed by the effects on charitable giving of the proposal to limit the deductible gift to the donor's cost (less expenses or costs already deducted). Without the two-pronged sweetener of avoidance of the tax on appreciated property—and especially stocks and bonds—and a charitable deduction for the full value of the property, they contend that large gifts to community chests, colleges, hospitals, and other exempt organizations would simply not be forth-coming in anything like their present magnitude.

These fund raisers admit, some of them bitterly, that the present law is unfair to the man who has no appreciated property to donate and contributes dollars shrunken by taxes; and that people in the entertainment field, who year after year contribute their talents generously to charity drives, have particular reason for resenting the tax discrimination they suffer. But my informants hold that if we withdraw the present tax incentives to gifts of property, we will jeopardize the existence and cripple the growth of exempt organizations. It would be shortsighted, in their view, to take such a step, for in the long run, Federal, state and local governments will have to bear the costs now borne by private organizations, which will far exceed the taxes lost through these loopholes.

Again, dear reader, we face a nice dilemma. Tax equality calls for putting an end to the allowance without tax of a charitable-contribution deduction for the full value of appreciated property. But the repeal of this tax-incentive to charitable giving may endanger essential community organizations that are supported by private contributions. While people in every industry tend to exaggerate the tax deterrents to their operations, my own observation of charitable giving leaves me with the uneasy feeling that tax considerations do play a large role in substantial gifts. In the circumstances, I would be inclined to compromise, albeit reluctantly, the tax-equality principle for expediency's sake, by allowing the present deduction for gifts of appreciated property.

Nevertheless, such a yielding of principle to the paramount need to encourage charitable gifts does not warrant acceptance of other devices we have considered. No one ought to make money at the Treasury's expense by giving a donation to an exempt organization; that's not merely an incentive, it's a bounty that we can be well rid of. Hence, the deduction now allowed, for example, for the value of a ten-year income interest under a trust under which the property will revert to the donor's family, ought to be eliminated from the statute. And Congress ought to act to insure that the courts will not overrule the Treasury as to the Pomona College device. These and other steps, including the administrative tightening up of valuations of gifts of property to charity, are needed to safeguard the revenues, without serious hurt to legitimate charitable giving. Charity ought to be blessed by the tax laws, but the blessings ought to be kept within reasonable bounds.

CHAPTER 12

Taxes and Morals

A cynic has suggested that there is some fraud in the heart of every taxpayer. Perhaps this is an exaggeration, but there is probably no criminal law on the books that more upright, respectable citizens violate each year than the law prohibiting wilful tax evasion (traffic violations, which would doubtless top all other infractions of the law, are typically "offenses," not crimes). I dare say that few taxpayers who have the opportunity to do so fail to chisel a bit here or there in their income-tax returns. Cutting corners on income-tax returns is socially acceptable; indeed, it's not uncommon to hear people boast of how they got away with this or that unwarranted deduction.

Perhaps the most fertile area available to business and professional men for being less than honest with the tax collector lies in the deduction of business expenses. Most of us err in our own favor in drawing the somewhat blurred legal line between personal and business expenses, in charging as tax deductible part of the expenses of cars, homes, theaters, restaurant and country-club bills, and travel in the United States and abroad. It has long been the practice to "estimate" many expenses for tax purposes (a practice that will be curtailed under the 1962 law's provisions requiring stricter accounting for travel and entertainment expenses).

There is, of course, often room for legitimate and honest controversy as to whether particular items are truly business expenses or personal items. On the audit of most

business men's returns, these issues are a standard item of
dispute. Nevertheless, from a good many years of meander-
ing through the tax field, in dealing with clients, friends,
revenue agents, accountants and lawyers, I am left with
the strong impression that most of us are aware that
we regularly and deliberately overstate our entertainment
and other business-expense deductions. And we likewise
tend to stray a bit from the straight and narrow path in
claiming "miscellaneous" charitable contributions.

There is also widespread evasion of tax liabilities through
failure to report taxable income. We have known for years
that there are large discrepancies between the amounts of
dividends paid by corporations and interest paid by savings
banks and the amounts that show up on income-tax returns.
A Treasury study of 1959 incomes estimated that individual
taxpayers failed to report in that one year some $940 million
in taxable dividends and $2.8 billion of taxable interest, with
a consequent revenue loss of $850 million.

It should be emphasized that we are not now discussing
"tax avoidance," by which we mean taking advantage of
provisions, loopholes, or privileges that the law grants to taxpayers. Nor are we dealing with the many borderline cases,
where there is legitimate controversy as to whether an item
is taxable or exempt from tax, or whether an item is deductible or nondeductible. Every taxpayer has a legal and
moral right to pay no more tax than Congress requires of
him under the law of the land. There should be no oppro-
brium attached to taking every advantage granted by Congress and employing every legal technique available to reduce one's tax liability. We are instead here concerned with
"tax evasion," the deliberate failure to report items that we
know are taxable, the conscious overstatement of deduc-

tions, and other infractions of the tax law that are reflected in the income-tax returns we file.

Apart from the "fudging" of the income tax that is within the accepted mores of decent, upright citizens, there are the flagrant tax-evasion devices that respectable members of our society frown on and do not often engage in. Every year there are tax-fraud prosecutions which bring to light cases of taxpayers who keep double sets of books, showing the tax collector one profit and hiding the rest; of business men who conceal large profits through grossly understated inventories; of income siphoned off from corporations without tax through elaborate and misleading book transactions. There are the recurring cases of doctors and dentists who pocket fees which never find their way into income-tax returns. No year passes without prosecutions of some individuals with large incomes who have simply filed no income-tax returns. And there are the corrupt politicians, the black marketeers and the gangsters whose exposure is compounded by their failure to report to the Treasury their ill-gotten gains.

Internal Revenue Service investigations have also disclosed free and easy deductions for nonexisting dependents claimed on returns as exemptions. Indeed, one of the new enterprises that has recently come to light is the corrupt "tax expert," who opens an office, often in a local drug store or barbershop, and for a small fee develops the art of claiming imaginary dependents for his clients. In 1959, two Brooklyn operators of such a tax-evasion service were sent to the penitentiary. In 1963, an operator of a Manhattan neighborhood tax service, who was neither an accountant nor a lawyer, was indicted for allegedly helping 2,000 taxpayers defraud the Government of about $350,000 by overstating deductions in their returns.

Moreover, the number of people who simply fail to file income-tax returns year after year is of large proportions. Two groups of taxpayers who are not subject to wage withholding are notorious for their failure to file returns—domestics and farm workers. A man or woman who employs a housekeeper or a maid is not required to withhold income tax, as does the business employer; and the farmer is not required to withhold taxes from the wages of his hired hands, apparently as a concession to the hardy individualism of the farmer and the political power of farm groups. The extension of the Social Security Act to domestics and agricultural employees in 1954 has resulted in reporting by employers of the wages of workers in these classes; but no correlation of the Social Security and income tax was made, with the result that large numbers of employees in those occupations continued to escape detection, although the facts were on record in Social Security files. However, the machine age is about to catch up with many of these nonfilers, through the Automatic Data Processing System, described below, that the Internal Revenue Service is now installing over the country.

Although the number of people, other than domestics and agricultural workers, who fail to file required returns and escape their income tax liabilities, is, doubtless, only a very small percentage of the number of returns filed, strange cases of nonfiling do show up. One of the most surprising cases on record is that of the tax specialist, a professor of taxation in a law school, who pleaded guilty in 1962, in the Federal District Court in Brooklyn, to failing to file his own tax returns.

Before pursuing our inquiry into our tax mores, it may be useful to outline the steps the Internal Revenue Service takes to police income-tax reporting. While our income-tax system has been widely regarded as a self-reporting, self-assessing system, this is true today only to a limited extent. During World War II, with the great broadening of the income-tax base, the Federal Government introduced the wage and salary withholding system. The Internal Revenue Service thus annually receives reports directly from employers of salaries and wages earned, along with taxes withheld at the first bracket, after allowance for exemptions and the standard deduction. Since wages and salaries account for more than four-fifths of all income reported on individual income-tax returns, most income of most taxpayers is reported to the Treasury by employers.

Moreover, to use 1960 as an example, when sixty-one million individual income-tax returns were filed, about 40 per cent used the short form prescribed for persons with gross incomes under $10,000, and not more than $200 of income not subject to withholding; and in 60 per cent of all returns, the standard deduction was used. There's little chance to cheat on the standard deduction, since it's a flat figure determined without reference to actual expenditures. Thus, by these devices, we have largely blocked off any substantial opportunity for the bulk of the taxpaying population to hide income or to overstate deductions. Indeed, without the wage and salary reporting and withholding by employers, it is open to question whether the mass-based income tax would not have broken down for noncompliance.

In 1962, the President asked Congress to extend the withholding system to recipients of dividends and interest. The failure to report billions of dollars of taxable interest and dividends has long been a chronic national problem. We have already noted that for 1959 more than $3 billion in taxable dividends and interest went unreported. This amounts to a sizeable portion of such income—an estimated 11 per cent of all dividends and over one-third of reportable interest. And the omission of taxable income is not confined to low-bracket, unsophisticated taxpayers, receiving small amounts of bank interest that are forgotten in the shuffle. One study disclosed that 70 per cent of the unreported dividends were received by individuals with incomes over $10,000, and that 30 per cent of the unreported interest was omitted from returns showing $10,000 or larger incomes. The withholding system offered a natural and easy way of enforcing collection of taxes escaped on dividends and interest.

A storm of protest broke over Capitol Hill when the withholding plan was proposed. Banks, savings and loan associations and corporations which would have the withholding job, widely circularized their depositors and stockholders, urging them to oppose the plan; local newspapers carried advertisements condemning the plan. Congressmen began to be deluged with mail, much of which was based on the misunderstanding that a new tax on dividends and interest was being proposed, a distortion which the financial institutions did little to dispel. The usually staid and contained Secretary of the Treasury, C. Douglas Dillon, delivered a blistering attack on the deprecators of withholding, referring to the "false arguments," "prejudiced mail" and the "new records for distortion" set in the campaign against the plan.

The informed arguments made against the withholding plan were that they would cause hardship to people who were not taxable and that they would have to file refund claims; that the whole procedure would be costly and cumbersome; and that it was not needed anyhow, because Automatic Data Processing would soon catch up with the delinquent taxpayers.

The Treasury undercut the hardship argument by presenting a plan for exemption certificates for persons who would not be taxable and for children under eighteen. The withholding would involve some expense, as all tax collection does, but the fact is that it would be less costly and more effective than information returns and the necessary Treasury efforts to collect the taxes due. An information reporting system merely provides the Treasury with information; it collects no taxes. The Treasury would have to correlate and follow up 250 million dividend and interest information returns a year to seek out delinquent taxpayers, whereas under a withholding system the taxes would be paid directly to the Treasury. The Commissioner of Internal Revenue reported that a dividend and interest information return system, without withholding, would require an inordinate amount of time, manpower and money in audit and follow-up procedures, and that the Treasury would actually collect only about 25 per cent of the taxes due, whereas a withholding system, less costly to operate, would bring in 80 per cent of the delinquent taxes.

The withholding plan, nevertheless, went down to defeat. The explanation undoubtedly lay, in the words of the President at a news conference, in the fact that "a great number of people have been badly misinformed." One Senator's mail bore this out eloquently; he had received 30,000 letters on withholding; between a third and a half of his irate correspondents thought withholding represented a new tax on dividends and interest. The sorry spectacle of respectable and conservative financial institutions all over the land lending their spirited efforts to the perpetuation of tax evasion and escape from taxation by their clients, and

in the process resorting to misleading propaganda and spe-
cious rationalization, did not serve to improve the tax
morality of the American people.

While the defeat of the withholding system for dividends
and interest will weaken the enforcement of the taxes on
these income sources, nevertheless the adoption of the payer
reporting system, coupled with the institution of the Automatic Data Processing System (ADP), should bring into
the tax net a substantial part of the dividends and interest
that now go unreported, as well as some other escaped income items.

ADP, a modern computer system designed to facilitate
the enforcement of the income tax, has been on the planning board for years, and its actual installation is now in
process. The IRS has long received millions of information
reports of salaries, wages, fees, interest and dividends of
$600 or more paid to any person; under the 1962 law,
interest and dividend payments of $10 or over must be re-
ported. The job of tieing in the information reports with
each taxpayer's record has been so costly and time consuming that this has been done in no more than 10 per cent to
15 per cent of the returns.

The electronic age will now make possible the collection
on magnetic tape of this information for all taxpayers in a
great national computer center at Martinsburg, West Vir-
ginia. Within a few years, the accounts of some seventy-
eight million taxpayers will be recorded on 400 miles of
magnetic tape, as a result of which the "Martinsburg Mon-
ster" will be able to produce at electronic speed any individual's tax profile. The huge machine, in a matter of sec-
onds, will flip out a card showing the returns filed, what
returns ought to have been filed, how much is owed, and
correlating information on all reports filed about the tax-

payer's income. ADP should eventually prove a great boon in tracking down delinquent taxpayers and tightening up the enforcement process.

Once the returns and information reports are in, the IRS begins its mammoth task of checking and reviewing. Returns are checked for mathematical errors. The IRS verdict is that our arithmetic is not all that it might be. In 1962, the Service's checkers found $135 million of errors in taxpayers' favor. But there were also $69 million in errors in the Government's favor; these taxpayers received refunds.

From this point on the reviewing process is greatly narrowed. Only a small fraction of the returns, about 5 per cent, are examined for verification of income and deductions, review of the propriety of the treatment of income as capital gain or ordinary income, and for the hundreds of controversial issues lurking in them. For 1962, about 3.2 million of the 61.5 million individual returns filed were audited by examining agents, either in IRS office audits or field examinations.

However, over the years the IRS has developed great skill in selecting returns for examination. Returns showing any unusual or doubtful transactions, taxpayers whose returns in prior years' audits produced substantial deficiencies, professions and businesses given to doubtful tax practices, spot checks of taxpayers, with variations from year to year to make sure that no particular taxpayer can comfortably rely on escaping audit—these are the techniques used by the Service. Naturally, returns with large incomes are more likely to be examined than those with small incomes. Nevertheless, large numbers of taxpayers have never been and never will be audited.

The experience of the Service is that auditing pays handsomely. In 1962, tax, interest and penalties assessed as a result of these audits totalled $1.9 billion. Of course, not all the taxes assessed were collected because of the assessments challenged and set aside, or compromised, as a result of legal proceedings brought by taxpayers.

Most audits are limited to ferreting out the taxpayer's deficiency (or refund); and it is to be observed that the Service will on its own initiative make refunds of overpaid taxes. It is the rare case that results in a criminal prosecution, since wilful failure to file returns or wilful evasion of tax are prerequisites for prosecution and criminal penalties. In 1962, about 125,000 leads suggesting possible tax frauds were screened and evaluated by the IRS; some 14,000 possible tax-evasion cases were considered, and about 3,500 full-scale investigations were conducted; 1,736 persons were indicted for tax frauds, and 1,146 convictions were obtained.

Measured by the millions of returns filed, the number of investigations conducted and prosecutions brought is miniscule, but their deterrent effects are undoubtedly far-reaching. On the other hand, the small number of investigations and prosecutions is not necessarily a fair gauge of the extent of undetected tax fraud, in view of the enormous number of returns that must go unaudited.

The flavor and variety of tax-fraud cases, which draw no class lines, are reflected in a sampling of the 1962 prosecutions. County Judge Woodrow Wilson Bean, of El Paso, Texas, who was defeated in a primary election runoff for U.S. Representative-at-large, was fined $5,000 and given a five-year suspended sentence for failing to file returns for five years. Among those convicted of tax evasion were Grant Foster, an American citizen living in Costa Rica, who was an international highway contractor; Jack Cooper, of Miami Beach, who purchased surplus military aircraft from Sweden and sold it to the Dominican Republic; Nathan Shavin, a

Chicago personal injury attorney; LaVere Redfield, a Nevada millionaire investor; a Chicago disc jockey; and a New Jersey insurance agent. Dave Beck, former President of the International Teamsters' Union, lost his appeal to the Supreme Court on his conviction for filing false information returns for a Seattle local, and began serving a five-year term.

There was in 1962 the usual complement of alleged racketeers, including Frank "Buster" Wortman of East St. Louis and his associate, Elmer "Dutch" Dowling, who were convicted of conspiring to evade income tax. A seventy-three-year-old Kansas swindler who failed to file on "borrowed" funds (he had "borrowed" over $170,000 in a thirty-year period), and a woman bookie were both jailed. A Seattle surgeon who was found guilty of tax evasion escaped prison when he agreed as part of his probation to serve a year in Nepal as a medical missionary for the United Medical Mission.

People are often puzzled as to how the Internal Revenue Service gets onto the trail of tax-fraud cases; we have already noted that 125,000 leads were considered in 1962. Sometimes a routine check of a return will disclose something suspicious that will result in a full-fledged inquiry. But other techniques are used. Newspapers are checked by the IRS for leads of all types; lawsuits between private parties often unwittingly reveal carefully hidden income; disclosures of corruption among public officials are likely to be followed by Treasury proceedings; convictions of gamblers and gangsters for nontax crimes may bring on a tax-fraud prosecution. The files of other government agencies are also often revealing sources of tax-fraud leads. The taxpayer who is in difficulty before the SEC, or whose charges under government contracts are under scrutiny may as a result find a Treasury agent on his trail. Perhaps the most startling and often the most revealing leads come from tips, sometimes anonymous, from disgruntled employees or discharged workers, from angered business associates, envious neighbors and jilted sweethearts. And there are those who inform to obtain the rewards the Treasury offers for information as to tax fraud. The Treasury's policy is to pay up to 10 per cent of the taxes and fines it collects as a result of informers' efforts; in 1962 the Treasury paid rewards of $587,000 to 665 informants through whose efforts it collected $13.5 million.

A case involving a Pasadena dental surgeon indicates the strange ways in which a tax-fraud prosecution may originate. The Los Angeles office of Internal Revenue received an anonymous telephone call, reporting that the dentist, Charles G. Wiggins, had understated his income, that he was away on vacation and that his books could be conveniently examined in his Pasadena office. IRS agents promptly descended on Dr. Wiggins' office, where they found in charge his nurse-secretary, who admitted that she had made the phone call. The record does not reveal what personal vengeful motives had led to the call; the informant had been the dentist's nurse-secretary for fifteen years. A dozen agents carefully examined the charts of 20,000 patients and the dentist's accounting records. When he returned from vacation, the stunned dentist, confronted with a mountain of incriminating evidence, confessed to his misdeeds.

These, then, are the methods used to police the income-tax system. At best, Treasury examination, auditing and investigation, civil and criminal, can detect only an insignificant number of infractions of the tax law. In the final analysis, especially for the 40 per cent of the taxpayers who file long-form returns and itemize their deductions—and these are the taxpayers whose incomes are typically above the national average—the effectiveness of our income-tax system depends essentially on voluntary compliance.

Despite the gaps and weaknesses in our voluntary reporting and the Lilliputian size of the Treasury's investigative force in grappling with its policing job, perhaps the most striking fact about our income-tax compliance is that we comply as smoothly and as effectively as we do. While it is true that some taxpayers fail to file returns or hide large income, that some engage in flagrant schemes of falsifying records, and that overstating deductions is an accepted national pastime, yet the stunning fact is that 97 per cent of the $99.4 billion of all taxes from all sources collected by the Federal Treasury in 1962 were voluntarily paid in by taxpayers, or were withheld at the source. As Commissioner of Internal Revenue Mortimer M. Caplin, who has brought a new personal touch and a warmth into Treasury communications, wrote in sending taxpayers their 1962 income-tax forms:

No other nation in the world has ever equalled this record. It is a tribute to our people, their traditions of honesty, and their high sense of responsibility in supporting our democratic form of government.

By way of contrast, the tax systems of a good many other countries have been enormously weakened, because it is fashionable in the "best" of circles to understate income, falsify records, overstate deductions and bribe tax officials to an extent that, whatever the shortcomings of our own tax morality, would shock most American communities. A weekly magazine some years ago printed that "Dodging the tax collector is almost a national sport in France and Italy. They are tax-ducking heavens for the upper brackets."

Put in this perspective, our income-tax mores stack up pretty well against those of other countries. But I do not believe that we can sink back into a comfortable feeling of complacency about our tax compliance, so long as tax chiseling is acceptable conduct. For, in addition to the moral issues that such conduct poses, loose tax-compliance practices create resentment at the whole income-tax structure among the millions of taxpayers who have no chance to cut the edges off their tax bills, and contribute to a general disregard of the law.

Why is income-tax chiseling respectable in our society? To start with the extreme cases—or to follow the clinical psychologist's method of illuminating normal behavior by studying abnormal conduct—the business or professional man who finds himself in the unfortunate position of being indicted and convicted of tax evasion is not really a "criminal" in our eyes. We certainly do not attach the same type of social stigma to a tax fraud conviction as we do to robbery or shoplifting. This is a "white collar" infraction of the law, like the derelictions of business men who were convicted of violating OPA price regulations during World War II, and the misconduct of employees of General Electric and Westinghouse recently sent to jail (for brief terms) for violating the antitrust laws. True, the person convicted of tax evasion is in disgrace in many quarters, but we hardly look on him as an antisocial character, who needs prison bars or psychiatric treatment to reorient him to be fit to live in our society.

By and large, a "soft" attitude toward tax fraud pervades our whole society. Thus, most judges mete out comparatively few substantial prison sentences to persons convicted of tax evasion, unless they are otherwise odious or disreputable characters, such as gamblers, gangsters or corrupt Government officials. Suspended prison sentences, with only fines are common even for cases involving large amounts of taxes evaded. Although tax evasion could bring a five-year sentence and a $10,000 fine for each offense, a study of forty-four tax-evasion cases prosecuted in the Federal District Court in Massachusetts from 1947 to 1953, in which the taxpayers pleaded guilty, reported that thirty-one received suspended sentences of two months to a year and a day, and fines of $200 to $5,000. One person was fined $1,000 and twelve were given jail sentences ranging between two months and eighteen months, the latter sentence having been meted out to an accountant. In 1963, an executive vice president of Manufacturers Hanover Trust Company, a large New York City bank, pleaded guilty to filing fraudulent returns for three years and evading $37,400 in taxes. He received no jail sentence, but was fined $18,000.

Light sentences in tax-evasion cases are not, of course, universal. Judges are unpredictable; their attitudes toward tax frauds vary; the coloration of the case and local regional sympathies and attitudes play their role. Thus, a Detroit surgeon enjoying a lucrative practice, who had failed to report $30,000 of income during two years, received a four-year prison term and a $10,000 fine. He had kept two sets of books, "black books" for the Government, and yellow pages recording his true receipts locked away in his private cabinet. A Tennessee businessman was sentenced to ten years in jail and a $40,000 fine, despite the fact that he was, in the words of the Court of Appeals, "of theretofore unblemished reputation, and a leader in his community."

By and large, however, the stiff sentences in tax-evasion cases, as is true with respect to white-collar crimes generally, tend to be reserved for disreputable characters, or persons who are regarded as evil on other scores. Thus, Joseph D. Nunan, Jr., former Commissioner of Internal Revenue, received a five-year sentence and a $15,000 fine for tax evasion, growing out of $160,000 of unreported and unexplained income during years that included his term as the nation's chief tax collector. One of the most severe income-tax sentences in recent years was meted out by a District Judge in St. Louis in what on its face, at least, measured by the tax evaded, was a picayune piece of tax evasion. Joseph W. Janko, who had been employed as a doorman and parking-lot custodian at a St. Louis night club, had claimed his two minor children as dependents, when he had not in fact supported them; his divorced wife had. Janko was in a low-income tax bracket, so that his false claim cut his taxes by only $134 for one year and $264 for another year. It is doubtful that he would ever have been indicted, except for the fact that he was linked with a notorious alleged St. Louis racket chief, Frank (Buster) Wortman. Janko received a ten-year sentence for his false dependency claims. The Supreme Court granted Janko a new trial because of newspaper articles, read by some members of the jury, describing the defendant as a "former convict" and "former employee of East Side rackets boss" Wortman.

The issue as to whether a man of high standing in the community who is convicted of income-tax evasion or other white-collar crimes should receive a comparatively light sentence touches on a controversy of far-reaching significance in the entire criminal law. There are varying philosophies as to the purposes and effects of criminal penalties— the reform of the wrongdoer, the protection of society against such conduct, deterrents to others, and a bit of social revenge. That controversy is, of course, beyond the province of this work, but the fact that judges are comparatively lenient in the run of the mill tax-evasion case is relevant to the community's moral evaluation of violations of the tax laws.

The judicial attitude towards tax fraud is also reflected in nontax cases that sometimes follow convictions under the tax laws. An alien who is convicted of a crime of moral turpitude may be deported from the United States. Some years ago, a Federal Circuit Court of Appeals held that an alien who had been convicted of evading the excise tax on whiskey could be deported because the crime involved moral turpitude. Judge Learned Hand, one of the luminaries of the American bench, in dissenting wrote:

I could wish that it was commonly thought more morally shameful than it is to evade taxes; but it is certainly true that people who in private affairs are altogether right-minded, see nothing more than a venial peccadillo in smuggling, or in escaping excises on liquor.

The lawyer and the accountant play a role in shaping our tax morality. As the advisers to business men and taxpayers in planning transactions, in preparing income-tax returns, in representing taxpayers before the IRS and the courts, the tax man cannot escape a virtually daily confrontation by moral issues—his client's and his own. There is no doubt that some lawyers and accountants encourage, are responsible for, and contribute to fraudulent tax schemes. All too frequently they are the intermediaries in corruption, the men who carry the little black bags to the Revenue Agent, or provide the vicuna coats for the wife of the corrupt higher-up official. And the books are full of cases in which the accountants and lawyers were the architects and engineers of their clients' misdealings. They are necessarily the brains of sophisticated tax frauds, their knowledge and skills are indispensable to the writing up of misleading book entries, and to the setting up of the contracts and other instruments through which the skullduggery is executed.

Responsible lawyers and accountants and their professional organizations roundly condemn these practices. Self-respecting lawyers and accountants do not engage in such conduct. We must not condemn the professions as a whole for the misconduct of the few. But there are other practices that are widely engaged in by respected and high-minded members of the bar and the accounting fraternity that fall short of the standards of morality that we have a right to expect. I refer to the distortions, the omissions and the half-truths that lawyers and accountants employ in dealing with the Internal Revenue Service on behalf of their clients; the misleading documents, the undisclosed "little side agreements," and the skillfully dressed up transactions, which are artfully set up so as to conceal the true nature of the transaction, without affirmatively misstating the facts.

To illustrate, a lawyer confronted by the possible assertion of an accumulated earnings tax against a corporation suggests to the board of directors that it adopt a resolution setting forth plans for the expansion of the business. Now, of course, almost any business can have some vague and undetermined plans for expansion; the resolution builds on this fact and seeks to create an impression of definite expansion intentions which do not in fact exist.

Or a lawyer prepares a bill for his legal fees for his client; he includes in the fees to the corporation controlled by the client the charges for handling the purchase of the client's house, or in obtaining a divorce for the client's daughter, without, of course, specifying these matters. The result, it is hoped, will be a business-expense deduction by the corporation for the client's personal, nondeductible expenses that are proper charges against him personally.

An accountant buries a capital or a nondeductible expenditure in an expense account of a business in a way that the Revenue Agents are not likely to ferret out. A lawyer submits a brief or memorandum to the Internal Revenue Service, which omits crucial facts known only to the client and to the taxpayer, hoping that the Internal Revenue Service will not stumble on them and thereby weaken or destroy the case.

These are the types of half-truths and omissions and distortions which recur, to a greater or lesser extent, in the practice of many of the most highly respected and leading members of the tax and acounting professions. We assuage our consciences by rationalizations; we're master rationalizers at the bar! We hide behind the traditional Anglo-American adversary system, under which each litigant is permitted to do his best to hide the skeletons in the closet of his case; the theory is that by cross-examination, the truth may emerge. We make much of the lawyer's obligation not to reveal the confidences of his client. We spend endless hours, and have developed great skill, in drafting contracts and resolutions and briefs with meticulous care so as to be able to avoid any actual misstatement of fact, while straining to create a misleading impression.

Nevertheless, the long and short of these artful techniques is distortion, half-truth and inadequate disclosure. Clients eye these works of lawyers with respect and admiration for our alchemy, and the whole process provides a professional stamp of approval for the client's own chicanery and concealment. All this strengthens and encourages the clients as to the social acceptability of chiseling on their tax returns.

This is the negative role which tax practitioners play; these practices hurt our tax morality. But the lawyers and the accountants at the same time perform a positive role that strengthens our tax morality. Over-all, these professions exercise an important restraining influence on the excesses of their clients. While lawyers are likely basically to reflect the tax ethics of the communities in which they live and of the business men and other taxpayers they represent, yet because of their training and experience in the law, their immersion in its traditions and values, lawyers are likely to have a deeper respect for tax compliance than most laymen. It may surprise laymen who have not dealt closely with tax lawyers to be informed that they spend a good deal of their time dissuading their clients from engaging in illegal and improper tax actions, at least actions that do not have some color of propriety. This may be due in part to the essential conservatism of the legal discipline, and to the greater fear of detection and the consequences of exposure among lawyers than among most business men. However, I like to think that exposure to the law and its teachings has something to do with the lawyers' role in preventing the more extreme types of misconduct among their clients. And many accountants perform a similar function.

One final note on the tax practitioner and tax morality. A wholesome development is beginning to take place in the legal and accounting professions. During the past ten years or more, there has emerged a new and deeper concern with the ethical problems of tax practice. Articles are being written, symposiums are being held and, indeed, a literature on the subject of tax ethics is beginning to grow up.

These are hopeful signs, for a sense of guilt about existing practices is a prerequisite to the improvement of accepted mores. Some tax lawyers have called for a recognition that a citizen's relation to his government, and in turn his lawyer's relations to government representatives in dealing with the client's tax return, is not comparable to that of two parties to a piece of private litigation, where each side has the essential facts at hand. If each citizen is to bear his fair share of the tax bill, ought he not be held to a standard of full and fair disclosure to the Government, which is a stranger to the income-producing transactions, of all the relevant facts? Should the accountant who prepares a re-turn be required to disclose all relevant facts, hurtful as well as helpful, that bear on the correct determination of the taxpayer's liability? While vigorously presenting every available legal argument, shouldn't the lawyer appearing before the Internal Revenue Service, or a court in a civil tax case, be subjected to the high duty of revealing all facts and documents relevant to the year's tax liability, whether or not a Revenue Agent has been able to dig them up from his examination of the records shown to him? Such stand-ards for the tax practitioner in civil tax matters have not yet gained wide acceptance in either profession. Conceivably, if a standard of full and fair disclosure were imposed as a condition to the preparation of income tax returns and of appearing in any civil tax proceeding, much of the loose practice now engaged in by tax practitioners of integrity would end. Taxpayers would come closer to paying the tax bill prescribed by Congress. And practitioners ought to be the first to welcome the imposition of such standards, for at least many tax men would thereby be relieved of the pangs of conscience they now regularly suffer.

A good many people not only agree, as is suggested by some judicial decisions, that infractions of the income-tax laws involve no act of moral turpitude; they go further and vigorously defend the payment of less tax than the law calls for. Perhaps I can best present this point of view by recalling a dinner party at my home some years ago at which the discussion eventually got around to cutting corners in income-tax returns. One of our guests, a high-minded and respected psychoanalyst, declared that he had no pangs of conscience whatever in overstating his business-expense deductions, because that's the only way he can come anywhere near paying his fair share of the income tax. Most people, he knows, "get away with murder," and chisel on a far larger scale than he does. He was particularly bitter about physicians who receive a substantial part of their fees in cash and don't report the income. As a psychoanalyst, unlike many physicians, he must give his patients receipts for their payments, because so many of them take medical-expense deductions. "Most of the Cadillacs and Continentals parked along New York's fashionable avenues are paid for at Uncle Sam's expense," he argued. "I'm not cheating Uncle Sam one bit when I overstate my deductions in my modest way. I'm merely correcting a small part of the injustice done me by lax enforcement of the tax laws. I'd be delighted to pay every penny the law calls for, if they'd really go after the big fish, because then everybody's rates would go down."

A building contractor took up the argument and accused us of being naive if we thought we could play the tax game honestly and get fair treatment. Our soirée took place not long after a Congressional Committee in 1953 had completed an investigation of the Internal Revenue administration and had exposed corruption reaching from the auditing field agents to the top officials. As a result of that investigation, former Commissioner of Internal Revenue Nunan was indicted and went to jail for tax evasion because of $160,000 of unexplained and unreported receipts.

The Assistant Attorney General in charge of the Tax Division of the Department of Justice, who had been in charge of prosecuting tax evaders, admitted accepting fur coats for his wife and daughter from a law firm handling a tax case before him, and of receiving large "commissions" in questionable business transactions from persons under a cloud as to taxes. He wound up in the penitentiary. Nine of the sixty-four Collectors of Internal Revenue over the country were removed from office or forced to resign, and two were sent to jail as a result of the investigation.

With all this fresh in our minds, and tales being heard on all sides of how taxpayer after taxpayer had settled his case by bribing a revenue agent, the building contractor added his own experiences in dealing with public officials in the construction business. "No building," he averred, "can be built without payoff. Every builder figures as part of his costs, graft payments that go from inspectors on the job right up to the chiefs. If you want to be a builder, you've got to pay graft, and if you want to get anything like a fair shake as a taxpayer, you've got to try to get by with everything you can on your tax return, and then be ready to take care of the revenue agent. Otherwise you'll wind up holding the bag."

An insurance consultant picked up the argument. He contended that the income-tax law is stacked against the professional and the little man in favor of businessmen and owners of stocks, bonds and other property. Big business and vested wealth, he argued, control Congress. They don't need to cheat on their returns (although, he argued, they rub salt into the wounds by doing that, too) because their tax loopholes have been legalized. He enumerated many of the areas we have considered in earlier chapters in this work, tax-exempt income, percentage depletion, capital gains,

stock options, family trusts and so forth, which serve to reduce the taxes of large corporations and of men of property
and wealth. The average man, who earns only service income, he contended, is discriminated against by the law
makers. While overstating deductions or omitting dividends
or interest income will not set things right, no one, he argued, can properly criticize the disfavored taxpayers from
using these devices to offset in a small measure the injustices
of the tax law.

These are impressive and troublesome arguments. They
do, however, raise a question crucial to the maintenance of
law and order in a democratic society. Our laws are made
by our elected legislative representatives, and enforced by
our elected executives and their appointees. If each of us
takes the law into his own hands, when dissatisfied with the
legislation enacted, or with its enforcement, anarchy will
result. Can we tolerate or approve the action of individual
citizens in flouting our tax laws or their enforcement?

The answer to this question is not an easy one, for there
are some laws whose open defiance we have tolerated and,
indeed, lauded as politically desirable. Thus, the action of
Northerners in pre-Civil War days in organizing the under-
ground railway to smuggle slaves out of the Southern states
to freedom in the North, in violation of the laws of the
Southern states (the famous Dred Scott decision held that
the slaves were still the property of their owners when they
reached the North), is now generally hailed as an heroic and
acceptable defiance of law. Since 1954, when the Supreme
Court's historic decision in the school-desegregation cases
was handed down, condemning the doctrine of equal but
separate schooling as a violation of the constitutional requirement of equal protection of the law, a large part of
the respectable citizenry in Southern communities has

placed obstacle after obstacle—legal and illegal—in the way of enforcement of this constitutional requirement; and these actions are vigorously supported by much of the Southern leadership.

Wholesale violations of the Volstead Act during prohibition days was condoned by our society. This scorning of law undoubtedly contributed to the adoption of the Twenty-First Amendment and the repeal of the prohibition legislation that was popularly regarded as an undue restriction on individual liberty. The refusal of ex-Communists to name their former comrades before the House un-American Activities Committee and the Senate Internal Security Committee, despite holdings of the Supreme Court that such action flouts the law, is applauded in some quarters of our society.

These illustrations of defiance of laws, which are not in keeping with the popular will in a particular community or in the entire nation, or which violate what many people regard as basic constitutional rights or liberties, could be multiplied. However, in examining these cases, one fact stands out—the entire legal institution involved, slavery or judicially enforced segregation, prohibition, the whole business of inquiry into political beliefs and associations, is regarded by many as an odious governmental act to be condemned and obstructed by every means available, including the flouting of the law. I do not believe that there are many citizens who will place the income tax in that category. By and large, the overwhelming majority of people recognize that the income tax is a desirable levy; that the principle of graduated rates, according to ability to pay, is an equitable and democratic one; and that it would be unthinkable to destroy this key fiscal measure of our national government. True, everybody has his own pet gripes about the tax. We have already mentioned the complaints of un-

fairness, discrimination and loose and corrupt enforcement.
And there are large groups who criticize the income tax
from a very different vantage point. They feel that the high
rates are confiscatory, that they undermine our capitalist
system by drying up the sources of new investment and by
stifling the profit motive, and that the income tax has made it
possible for government to extend its powers and functions
to private sectors of our economy (TVA is a prime example), and has encouraged the welfare state and socialistic
measures, which threaten our capitalistic system. Some
people support a constitutional amendment to put a ceiling
of 25 per cent on Federal income-tax rates. Yet, it is highly
significant that not even the most extreme groups that have
any substantial following in the nation call for a repeal of
the income tax (there are a few isolated voices here and
there, such as the followers of Henry George's single-tax
policy, who do call for repeal of the income tax; but they
have no substantial support). We have not had income-tax
strikes, comparable to the Poujadist tax-strike movement in
France. Consequently, after all our complaints are in, the
overwhelming majority of the American people are con-
vinced that they must keep the income tax and keep it
vital and strong.

Given a law whose continuation we approve, a law that
provides the financial lifeblood of our government and our
national security, the citizen in a democratic society has no
choice, I believe, but to support the law and seek changes
in the tax by lawful means; by electing representatives who
will work for the desired modifications, and by electing executives who will enforce the law effectively. Because a cyni-
cal attitude towards the income tax threatens this basic and
essential fiscal institution of the national government, a
citizen of integrity ought not be satisfied to justify his own

chiseling, because the other fellow gets away with flagrant cheating, or because he regards the law as oppressive, or unfairly drawn, or badly enforced.

I am not expecting even people of integrity and high standards to be income-tax saints. My experience is that such persons are as hard to find in our society as honest men in Diogenes' world. Most decent people I meet have normal human frailties; but I do think that we ought not delude ourselves into rationalizing our income-tax offenses as anything less than derelictions. We ought at least feel a twinge of conscience when we omit taxable income. We ought to suffer feelings of guilt that cannot be assuaged by the justifications offered in their defense. In such an operation of a democratic society's superego, to borrow a Freudian term, lies the hope for a society of law and order and for a lifting of our standards of tax morality.

ABOUT THE AUTHOR

Jerome Hellerstein was born in Denver, Colorado. He attended the University of Denver, received his M.A. at the State University of Iowa and his L L.B. from the Harvard Law School. In 1938 he was appointed Assistant Corporation Counsel handling taxes for the City of New York. In 1946 he formed a law firm in which he specializes in taxation.

Since 1959 Mr. Hellerstein has been Professor of Taxation at N.Y.U. Law School and has lectured at tax institutes all over the country. He is the author of *State and Local Taxation: Cases and Materials,* which is used in law school courses, and he has contributed to the Encyclopaedia Britannica. Mr. Hellerstein is married and has four children.